THE LEAGUE OF NATIONS
AND THE GREAT POWERS

THE
LEAGUE OF NATIONS
AND THE
GREAT POWERS

THE GREEK-BULGARIAN INCIDENT, 1925

JAMES BARROS

CLARENDON PRESS · OXFORD

1970

949.77
B277

Oxford University Press, Ely House, London W.1

GLASGOW NEW YORK TORONTO MELBOURNE WELLINGTON
CAPE TOWN SALISBURY IBADAN NAIROBI DAR ES SALAAM LUSAKA
ADDIS ABABA BOMBAY CALCUTTA MADRAS KARACHI LAHORE
DACCA KUALA LUMPUR SINGAPORE HONG KONG TOKYO

PRINTED IN GREAT BRITAIN
BY W & J MACKAY & CO LTD, CHATHAM

To
Andrew and Alexis

PREFACE

THE Greek-Bulgarian Incident of 1925 has often been pointed to as the League of Nations' greatest political success during the inter-war years. Unfortunately, the inaccessibility of archival materials in the past made impossible any serious study of this important inter-war episode in international coercion. The two works written a few years after the incident are inadequate: the first is mostly the reminiscences of *Le Matin*'s Sofia correspondent;[1] while the second is largely a nationalist tract.[2]

The passage of almost forty-five years, however, has made available a number of archival materials previously closed to investigation. The study of these papers has made it possible to view the incident in a clearer light. By doing so, the actions of the Great Powers and the true role of the League of Nations are exposed. Likewise, additional light is thrown on how and why the League was able to score such a great success in 1925; the success in turn giving us a greater insight into the possibilities and limitations of coercion and peaceful settlement under the aegis of international organization.

[1] Felix de Gérando, *L'Incident Gréco-Bulgar d'Octobre 1925* (Sofia, 1926).

[2] Georges V. Saraïlieff, *Le Conflit Gréco-Bulgar d'Octobre 1925 et son Règlement par la Société des Nations* (Amsterdam, 1927).

ACKNOWLEDGEMENTS

No study of this type could have been made without the aid and assistance of numerous people. I would therefore like to express my gratitude to Mr. A. C. Breycha-Vauthier, the former Director of the United Nations Library at the Palais des Nations in Geneva, who gave me permission to examine and quote from the Archives of the League of Nations; to Lord Salter and Dr. Adrian Joost van Hamel for permission to reproduce their memoranda; to Mr. K. W. Humphreys, Librarian of the University of Birmingham, who allowed me to examine and quote from the papers of Sir Austen Chamberlain; to Professors Mario Toscano and Renato Mori, who opened for my inspection the Archives of the Italian Foreign Ministry; to the personnel of the Public Record Office in London and the National Archives of the United States in Washington, D.C., who assisted me in my examination of the Archives of the British Foreign Office and the United States Department of State; to Mr. Constantine Hadzithomas, the former Director of the Archives Division of the Greek Foreign Ministry, and his associates, Mr. Epaminondas Ekonomidis and Mr. Constantine Pantelidis, as well as to the Director of the Greek Parliamentary Library, Mr. Alcibiades Provatas, and the historian, Angelo Papacosta, for their valuable assistance.

Finally, I would like to thank the American Philosophical Society of Philadelphia, the Dartmouth College Committee on Research, and the Humanities and Social Sciences Division of the Rockefeller Foundation, whose support made this study possible. A special note of thanks is due to the Society for allowing me to reproduce certain sections which appeared in its proceedings.

Needless to state, any views herein are my own and in no way reflect the views or opinions of the people or organizations which have supported me in this endeavour.

JAMES BARROS

Department of Political Economy
Erindale College
University of Toronto

CONTENTS

ABBREVIATIONS

CHAMBERLAIN PAPERS   The Personal Papers and Letters of Sir Austen Chamberlain, University of Birmingham Library, Birmingham, England.

GREEK ARCHIVES   The Archives of the Greek Foreign Ministry, Athens.

ITALIAN ARCHIVES   The Archives of the Italian Foreign Ministry, Rome.

LEAGUE OF NATIONS ARCHIVES   The Archives of the League of Nations, United Nations Library, Palais des Nations, Geneva.

NA   The Archives of the Department of State and the Archives of the German Foreign Ministry, National Archives of the United States, Washington, D.C.

PRO   The Archives of the British Foreign Office, the Public Record Office, London.

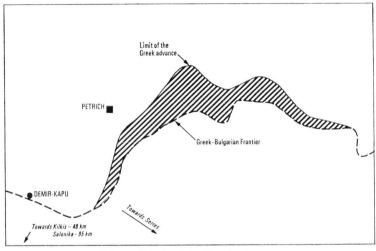

MAP 1 Limit of the Greek advance

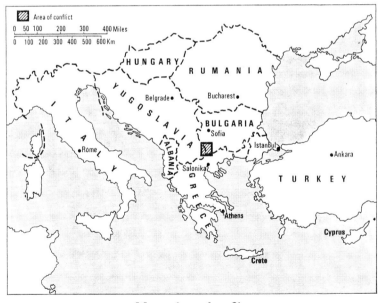

MAP 2 Area of conflict

I

A BORDER INCIDENT

Distorted Messages

THE autumn of 1925 appeared to have ushered in a new Europe. On 16 October, after long negotiations the Locarno Pacts had been signed, establishing the Franco-Belgian-German frontiers and re-admitting Germany, after a decade, once more into the family of nations. For the moment Europe was at peace. Even in the Balkans, that cockpit of European politics, there was peace.

Thus the border incident that occurred on the early afternoon of 19 October,[1] near Demir-Kapu, a remote section of the Greek-Bulgarian frontier, for a while went unnoticed by the Allied representatives at Sofia.[2]

Conflicting accounts make it difficult to pinpoint responsibility for the incident. The only facts definitely established by subsequent investigation were that on the early afternoon of 19 October, in an exchange of shots, a Greek border sentry was killed and a Greek officer arriving at the scene, ostensibly to effect a cease-fire, was also killed. Shooting along the border became general and the

---

[1] According to the Bulgarians the incident erupted at 1.30 p.m.; according to the Greeks at 2.45 p.m. Report of the Commission of Enquiry into the Incidents on the Frontier between Bulgaria and Greece. Text. League of Nations, *Official Journal*, 7th year, 1926, p. 198.

[2] The first inkling the Bulgarian public had that anything was amiss on the frontier was the sketchy press reports that appeared on 21 October, two days after the incident. (Rosetti (Sofia) to the F. Min., no. 1756, 21 Oct. 1925. Greek Archives.) It was on this same day, 21 October, that the British Consulate-General in Salonika informed the British Legation in Athens and the Foreign Office of what had occurred. The legation then in turn also informed the Foreign Office. (Salonica to Athens, no. 6, repeated to the F.O., 21 Oct. 1925. File 953, FO/286/916, PRO; Cheetham (Athens) to the F.O., no. 159, 21 Oct. 1925. File 13309, FO/371/10672, PRO.)

The surprise of the Allied representatives on the morning of 22 October was complete. No one had realized during the preceding days that what had started out as a simple frontier incident would mushroom into a Greek invasion of Bulgaria. (Cable (Sofia) to the Dept. of State, 25 Oct. 1925. File 768.74/232, Record Group 59, NA.)

Greek troops were forced to evacuate their exposed border post.[3]

First news of the skirmish reached Athens in the early morning of 20 October. It was that time of the year when komitadji bands usually descended from the mountains and congregated in the plains in and around the Bulgarian border city of Petrich. During this same period the Greek military along the Greek-Bulgarian border had ascertained that the komitadjis were trying to find out the strength of the Greek frontier posts and had discovered that they were largely under strength, as the Greek troops had been given leave in order to vote in the coming municipal elections. Consequently news of the frontier incident caused the Greek commanders on the spot to jump to the conclusion, as the Greek Minister in London, Demetrios Caclamanos, subsequently explained, 'that this was an advance in force by komitajis, who intended to seize the passes of Kula and Ruppel and descend towards the sea'.[4] In retrospect the communication sent to Athens that the 'incident was premeditated by the Bulgarians' is therefore understandable, but it established the atmosphere of mistrust that was to pervade the Greek Ministry of War that morning.

In an earlier report from Demir-Kapu the Intelligence Officer of the covering battalion had communicated to his commanding officer that, '*according to information*, Bulgarian forces *amount to one battalion*', and that the Bulgars were equipped with machine-guns. This news, however, was transmitted to the War Ministry in an altered form, so that it read 'Bulgarians have *attacked*' in battalion strength and were occupying the hilltop. Unfortunately, no attempt was made by the Ministry to verify this information. Feeling, no doubt, that this was a premeditated Bulgarian attack in considerable strength, and anxious about its communications with Thrace, which were precarious in that area (the railway line ran parallel to the Bulgarian frontier at a distance less than 6.25 miles

---

[3] Report of the Commission of Enquiry into the Incidents on the Frontier between Bulgaria and Greece, loc. cit., p. 198. The Bulgarians alleged that the Greek sentry was killed in Bulgarian territory, while the Greeks maintained that the Bulgarians had dragged the corpse into their territory. As to the officer's death, accounts again differ. The Greeks assert that upon arrival the officer had ordered the Greek troops to cease fire and had advanced under a white flag, at which point he was shot. The Bulgarian version was that they saw neither the white flag nor the officer, that the Greeks had not ceased firing, and that the officer was killed by a bullet not aimed at him.

[4] Record of a Conversation between Mr. Howard Smith and M. Caclamanos, 30 Oct. 1925. File 13309, FO/371/10673, PRO.

from it), the Ministry of War, on receipt of this message, ordered the 3rd and 4th Army Corps to prepare an advance into Bulgaria via the Struma Valley.[5]

What started out as a simple frontier incident had, because of faulty intelligence and distorted messages, escalated into a serious situation. Events during these early hours had moved with such breath-taking speed that they sealed beforehand the fate of the diplomatic moves between Athens and Sofia.

Bulgarian Proposals in Sofia and Athens

On the Bulgarian side, news of the firing at Demir-Kapu reached the General Staff at about 5 p.m. on the afternoon of 19 October. It was considered as merely another border incident, of the kind endemic to the Balkans, and instructions were transmitted to terminate the skirmish; the General Staff gave it no further thought.[6]

In the case of the Royal Bulgarian Ministry of Foreign Affairs, information of what had transpired at the border was received only at 2.30 p.m. the following day. When the news arrived the Secretary-General of the Ministry, Constantine Minkoff, requested an interview with the Greek chargé d'affaires, Raoul Rosetti-Bibica. On Rosetti's arrival at the Foreign Ministry, Minkoff explained the occurrences at the frontier and requested that the Greek Government and the military authorities at Salonika be immediately informed in order that the Greek troops should cease fire. He also requested that the Greeks contact the Bulgarians at the border in order to ascertain the causes and responsibilities for the incident. Instructions to this effect were also forwarded to the Bulgarian Legation in Athens.[7] In an urgent message to the Greek Foreign Ministry the chargé recounted his discussion with the Secretary-General of the Foreign Ministry and added that, according to Minkoff, though Bulgarian officers had repeatedly raised the white flag to effect a cease-fire, the Greek troops had continued shooting. Concluding his report, Rosetti begged that Athens give immediate orders to the military of the kind desired by the Bulgarian Foreign

---

[5] Report of the Commission of Enquiry into the Incidents on the Frontier between Bulgaria and Greece, loc. cit., pp. 200–1.

[6] Ibid., p. 202.

[7] Ministère des Affaires Étrangères (Bulgarie), Récapitulation des événements concernant l'incident gréco-bulgare de Demir-Kapia jusqu'au moment de l'intervention du Conseil de la Société des Nations. Political 1925, League of Nations Archives.

Ministry.[8] At 8 p.m. that night, after filing his message to Athens, and undoubtedly attempting to reassure the Bulgarians, Rosetti informed the Foreign Ministry by telephone that he had telegraphed to his government as Minkoff had requested him to.[9]

At the same time that Rosetti's message was speeding towards Athens, other messages on the same subject were making their way to the Bulgarian Legation in the Greek capital. These messages from Sofia, after describing the incident and Minkoff's interview with Rosetti, instructed the legation to make representations to the Greek Government similar to those made to Rosetti, insisting that the Greek authorities at the frontier receive orders to establish contact with their Bulgarian counterparts. Acting on these instructions, the Bulgarian chargé d'affaires, Ivan Dantcheff, on the morning of 21 October requested an interview with the Greek Foreign Minister, Admiral Alexandros Hadjikyriakos. The interview took place at noon.[10]

Hadjikyriakos, 'whatever his capacity as a naval officer', wrote the British Minister in Athens, Sir Milne Cheetham, was 'by both temperament and education hardly fitted to deal with questions of diplomacy'. In this respect he was more than matched by the Prime Minister, General Theodoros Pangalos, who several months before, in late June, had assumed control of the government by a *coup d'état*. From the moment the incident erupted both the British and French Ministers in Athens found it difficult to make Pangalos 'understand the serious character of the situation', should the Athens government 'put themselves in the wrong by neglecting the advice given to them' by London and Paris. Pangalos 'viewed the situation from a military standpoint' and it was only gradually that he could be brought to comprehend that he might spoil the Greek case, which had its points, if he persisted in advancing the Greek Army into Bulgaria. Hadjikyriakos subsequently admitted that personally he had been opposed to the adventure of which no one could guess the outcome. Pangalos insisted, however,

[8] Rosetti (Sofia) to the F.Min., no. 1746, 20 Oct. 1925. Greek Archives.

[9] Ministère des Affaires Étrangères (Bulgarie), Récapitulation des événements concernant l'incident gréco-bulgare de Demir-Kapia jusqu'au moment de l'intervention du Conseil de la Société des Nations. Political 1925, League of Nations Archives.

[10] Ministère des Affaires Étrangères (Bulgarie), Sur les démarches faites par le Chargé d'Affaires de Bulgarie à Athènes auprès du Gouvernement hellénique au sujet de l'incident de frontière gréco-bulgare du Octobre 1925. Political 1925, League of Nations Archives.

that unless the 'Bulgarian aggression were dealt with promptly and with a strong hand', the Greek refugees from Asia Minor, who had been settled near the Bulgarian frontier and were already nervous, would flee to Salonika and the entire refugee problem would be greatly complicated. Faced with this argument, Hadjikyriakos 'had consequently given way'.[11]

As arrangements were being made for the Dantcheff-Hadjikyriakos interview, the Bulgarian Legation submitted to the Greek Foreign Ministry a very urgent *note verbale* in line with the instructions it had received from Sofia. The note pointed out that, though the incident had broken out two days before, firing continued in spite of the efforts of the Bulgarian authorities, who had hoisted the white flag a number of times in an attempt to contact their opposite number. The legation asked therefore that the Foreign Ministry intervene immediately so that orders could be transmitted without delay to the Greek border authorities to effect a cease-fire and to contact quickly their Bulgarian counterparts. In ending, the legation reserved the 'right to make further *démarches* in connection with the responsibilities springing from the . . . incident'.[12]

In his interview with Hadjikyriakos, Dantcheff repeated the Bulgarian requests and pointed out that the 'continuation and the eventual extension of the shooting could complicate the situation and lead to results contrary to the interests of the two countries'. The Foreign Minister ignored this comment and observed that the situation was grave because the attack appeared 'premeditated and prepared for long since', and had been executed by an unusual number of regular troops comprising about a battalion of the Bulgarian Army. He felt that the assault had not been provoked from the Greek side, and that the Bulgarian assailants, after having killed the Greek sentry and the Greek officer who had advanced under a white flag, had penetrated and occupied a large area of Greek territory. If it had merely been an armed attack perpetrated by 'irregulars and irresponsibles' (i.e. komitadjis), the event would have been far less serious. However, in view of the gravity of the situation and given the overexcited state of mind of the troops in the threatened region, the Greek Government thought itself obliged

[11] Cheetham (Athens) to Chamberlain, no. 338, 30 Oct. 1925. File 953, FO/286/916, PRO.
[12] *Note verbale* from the Bulgarian Legation to the Greek Foreign Ministry, dated 21 Oct. 1925. French Text. Greek Archives.

to 'give full powers to the military authorities of the region in question to undertake all measures which could be judged necessary in order to assure their security and that of the national territory'. At this point Hadjikyriakos enumerated the demands that would form the basis of Greece's subsequent note to Bulgaria. He stressed that the Greek Government, feeling that its national honour had been injured and that it was only just to grant indemnities to the families of the slain men, hoped that the Bulgarian Government would consent to the following: to inflict an exemplary punishment on the military commanders responsible; to express its regrets to the Greek Government; and lastly, to pay an equitable indemnity of six million drachmas to the families of the slain men. To these demands the Greek Government desired an immediate response. Almost as an afterthought, he added that it was possible that the Greek troops in the Salonika region, unaware of the 'designs and intentions of the Bulgarian troops', might deem it necessary 'to proceed to the occupation of certain strategic points of Bulgarian territory', so as to ensure their own security, endangered by the Bulgarian attack.

In reply, Dantcheff maintained that on the basis of the information which he had received from Sofia 'it was a question of a simple frontier incident' and that a mixed commission of inquiry could easily establish the causes and responsibilities involved. Besides, he observed, in many cases of a similar nature, his government had always insisted on the need to proceed with preliminary inquiries in order to establish responsibility and that this was the way indicated for the settlement of the border incident which had arisen. Though he would, of course, communicate the Greek view to his government, he insisted again on the need to effect an immediate cease-fire on the Greek side and to order the competent authorities to establish contact with the Bulgarian officers at the border.

Concluding the interview, the Foreign Minister promised Dantcheff that he would transmit to the Prime Minister, General Pangalos, the requests of the Bulgarian Government and would contact him accordingly.[13]

While this discussion was going on in Athens, in Sofia, Rosetti

---

[13] Ministère des Affaires Étrangères (Bulgarie), Sur les démarches faites par le Chargé d'Affaires de Bulgarie à Athènes auprès du Gouvernement hellénique au sujet de l'incident de frontière gréco-bulgare du Octobre 1925. Political 1925, League of Nations Archives.

once more appeared at the Bulgarian Foreign Ministry. It was his second interview with Minkoff within twenty-four hours. He was informed by the Secretary-General that shooting on the frontier had subsided and that the Bulgarian Government had appointed officers and begged that the Greek Government do likewise, so that responsibility for the incident could be settled 'in [a] spirit [of] complete sincerity'.[14] Later in the day Rosetti was again recalled to the Foreign Ministry. In the interval the situation had deteriorated. According to Minkoff, since two o'clock that afternoon Bulgarian officers had been waiting at the border to meet with their Greek opposites. Unfortunately, shooting had again broken out and become general. Because of this, Sofia wanted settlement of the incident by an investigatory committee. Minkoff assured Rosetti that the Bulgarian military had been given strict orders to avoid any friction with the Greeks and to maintain only a defensive position. In ending the meeting he again begged that the Greek military be given orders to restore peace on the border in order that a settlement should be made possible.[15]

Late that night, Rosetti was visited by the British chargé d'affaires, Ralph C. S. Stevenson. Informed of the resumption of fire at the frontier, he had called seeking further information. The only additional details that Rosetti could offer were those he had dispatched to Athens. His English colleague then desired to know what 'official information' he had reflecting Greek views. Rosetti explained that he lacked instructions, but he 'attempted to explain and convince' Stevenson that the incident, as always, derived from Bulgarian responsibility because of the continued efforts of komitadji bands to cross the Greek frontier. During the present period many such crossings had been reported, with the komitadjis then committing murder on Greek territory. On this occasion, this was precisely what had happened. Though Stevenson 'accepted this interpretation', he observed that among foreign correspondents in Sofia, the belief was circulating that the Greek Government, finding itself in internal difficulties, had invited the border clash for the 'diversion [of Greek] public opinion'. This story Rosetti characterized as 'vile fancy', denying it categorically.

Stevenson appeared convinced by Rosetti's denials, but did not hide the fact that the story about Greek internal difficulties, if

[14] Rosetti (Sofia) to the F.Min., no. 1747, 21 Oct. 1925. Greek Archives.
[15] Rosetti (Sofia) to the F.Min., no. 1755, 21 Oct. 1925. Greek Archives.

circulated abroad, would be likely to be believed. In leaving, he added that he would communicate with London and the British Legation in Athens regarding the incident.[16]

As good as his word, Stevenson communicated to both the British Legation in Athens and the Foreign Office in London what had occurred, as well as Minkoff's requests to Rosetti and the latter's communications to Athens.[17] Rosetti, he subsequently explained to London, had also informed him that he had received neither instructions nor information from Athens, despite his three communications at the request of the Bulgarians expressing Sofia's desire for a joint investigation of the affair. Rosetti 'was at a loss to understand' the attitude of the Athens government and 'appeared distinctly anxious'. He told Stevenson that although he had not heard Athens's side of the story and could therefore form no opinion as to the original responsibility for the incident he was satisfied that the Bulgarians 'were genuinely anxious' to find a peaceful end to the affair.[18]

While this discussion was taking place in Sofia, proposals similar to those made to the Greek chargé by Minkoff were being repeated to Dantcheff in Athens. According to Sofia's instructions, Dantcheff was to propose the nomination of a Greek-Bulgarian mixed commission of inquiry with a view to ascertaining the responsibility for the incident and punishing the guilty. He was also charged to bring to the attention of the Greek Foreign Ministry that, until the evening of 21 October, no Greek officer had presented himself at the border to put an end to the shooting in conjunction with the Bulgarian officers there. Regardless of the absence of the Greek officers, the Bulgarian military had received strict instructions not

[16] Rosetti (Sofia) to the F.Min., no. 1758, 22 Oct. 1925. Greek Archives.

Stevenson's reference to Greek 'internal difficulties' was undoubtedly an allusion to General Pangalos's dictatorial government and the increasing resistance to it by the Greek populace.

The theory that internal difficulties in Greece had dictated the moves of the Greek Government was repeated by the American Legation in Sofia, and believed in Berlin. (Cable (Sofia) to the Dept. of State, 22 Oct. 1925. File 768.74/212, Record Group 59, NA; Memorandum on the Greek-Bulgarian Conflict submitted to the State Secretary, Berlin, 26 Oct. 1925. Microfilms of the German Foreign Ministry Archives 1920–45, Serial Number L39, Roll 4021, Frame Number L011158, NA.)

[17] Sofia to Athens, addressed to the F.O., no. 75, 21 Oct. 1925. File 953, FO/286/916, PRO.

[18] Stevenson (Sofia) to Chamberlain, no. 231, 28 Oct. 1925. File 13309, FO/371/10673, PRO.

to fire and to defend themselves only in the case of attack.[19]

Simultaneously, the Bulgarian Missions in Belgrade, Bucharest, London, Paris, and Rome were ordered to inform their respective governments of the representations and propositions made by the Bulgarian Government to Athens.[20] The dispatch of these orders perceptibly widened the international scope of what had until this point been solely a Greek-Bulgarian affair.

[19] Ministère des Affaires Étrangères (Bulgarie), Sur les démarches faites par le Chargé d'Affaires de Bulgarie à Athènes auprès du Gouvernement hellénique au sujet de l'incident de frontière gréco-bulgare du Octobre 1925. Political 1925, League of Nations Archives.

[20] Ministère des Affaires Étrangères (Bulgarie), Récapitulation des événements concernant l'incident gréco-bulgare de Demir-Kapia jusqu'au moment de l'intervention du Conseil de la Société des Nations. Political 1925, League of Nations Archives.

II

THE GREEK INVASION

The Greek Note

DURING this period events were also unfolding in the Greek Foreign Ministry. Fortuitously, the incident at the border had erupted at a moment when the Foreign Ministry found itself without a responsible, experienced, and talented minister. In a disagreement over a question of internal policy, Constantine Rentis, the Foreign Minister, had resigned a few hours before the news of the incident reached Athens. Informed at Corinth of what had happened, he returned to resume his post. In the interim, however, his position had become untenable by the publication of the private and confidential letter in which he had tendered his resignation to the Prime Minister, General Pangalos. The terms of Rentis's letter made it impossible for him to resume his former position as Foreign Minister. Thus the Foreign Ministry 'had remained for twenty-four hours or more without a responsible head . . . [and there] had therefore been nobody at that critical moment at the Foreign Ministry to weigh the political consequences of the Greek action'.[1] As Rentis himself later admitted, 'no one knew whether he was coming back or not; consequently, matters had drifted in the absence of a responsible chief'. He noted that his first move, had he been present, 'would have been to see that there was no violation of treaty engagements', referring to the Covenant of the League of Nations.[2]

Rentis's inability to resume his post as Foreign Minister explains Hadjikyriakos's appointment. But Rentis's absence did not mean that there was no voice for moderation raised within the Foreign Ministry. Indeed, the desire for moderation was mirrored in the

---

[1] Rumbold (Geneva) to Chamberlain, 1 Dec. 1925. File 13309, FO/371/10673, PRO; Record of a Conversation between Sir Austin Chamberlain and M. Rentis, 12 Dec. 1925. File 13309, FO/371/10673, PRO; Athens to the F.O., no. 161, 22 Oct. 1925. File 953, FO/286/916, PRO.

[2] Record of a Conversation between Sir Austen Chamberlain and M. Rentis, 12 Dec. 1925. File 13309, FO/371/10673, PRO.

actions of its Secretary-General, Lysimachos Caftanzoglou. Unfortunately, as the British Minister in Athens, Cheetham, noted to
London, Caftanzoglou had 'practically no experience or influence'.[3]
Nevertheless his attitude was to be symptomatic of the attitude of
his colleagues serving in Bern, Paris, and Sofia, who during the
coming days would plead with Athens for moderation and for a
policy based on the realities of Greece's weakness and international
position. Caftanzoglou, it appears, managed with great difficulty to
convince the Prime Minister, General Pangalos, of the dangers of
an ultimatum and felt that his insistence on moderation had avoided
one; yet the note delivered late on the evening of 21 October to the
Bulgarian Legation was for all intents and purposes still an ultimatum.[4] This note was also forwarded to Rosetti for delivery to the
Bulgarian Government with copies to the Greek Missions in
Belgrade, Berlin, Bucharest, London, Paris, and Rome.[5]

The note sent from the Foreign Ministry to the legation protested in the 'most energetic fashion' against the incident for which
Bulgaria was held entirely responsible. To the Greeks the incident
was an 'unqualified aggression'. The note then quickly recounted

[3] Athens to the F.O., no. 161, 22 Oct. 1925. File 953, FO/286/916, PRO.
[4] Facendis (Athens) to Mussolini, 22 Oct. 1925. Italian Archives; Schoen
(Athens) to the Wilhelmstrasse, 23 Oct. 1925. Microfilms of the German Foreign
Ministry Archives 1920–45, Serial Number L39, Roll 4021, Frame Number
Lo11174, NA.
    That Caftanzoglou did not consider the note sent to Bulgaria an ultimatum is
puzzling. According to Sir Harold Nicolson, *Diplomacy* (2nd ed., Oxford
University Press, 1950), p. 242, an ultimatum does not necessarily mean war; 'it is
often merely "the last word" before negotiation is broken off. It generally takes
the form of a written intimation that unless a satisfactory reply is received by a
certain hour on a certain date certain consequences will follow.' Sir Ernest N.
Satow, *A Guide to Diplomatic Practice*, ed. Nevile Bland (4th ed., Longmans,
Green and Co., 1957), p. 105, states that an ultimatum 'ordinarily but not always
implies a threat to use force, if the demand is not complied with'. However, a
more detailed examination is to be found in L. Oppenheim, *International Law*,
ed. H. Lauterpacht (7th ed., Longmans, Green and Co., 1952), II, p. 295, who
divides ultimatum into *simple* or *qualified*. The *simple* ultimatum does not include
any indication of the measures envisaged by the power or powers transmitting it.
On the other hand, a *qualified* ultimatum indicates measures envisaged, whether
reprisals, occupations, war, etc. The Greek note therefore would appear to fall
under the category of a *simple* ultimatum. But it should have been obvious to
Caftanzoglou that any note containing a series of demands, with a twenty-four-
hour time limit, sent by one of the victorious powers in the World War to one of
the defeated and virtually demilitarized powers, and a country with which
Greece had strained relations, had implied sanctions attached and was therefore
an ultimatum.
[5] *Le Messager d'Athènes*, 22 Oct. 1925, p. 4.

the Athens version of the incident: that on the nineteenth, Bulgarian border posts 'unexpectedly and without provocation' had commenced fire, killing a Greek sentry; that firing along the line became general and when the officer of the covering company arrived to effect a cease-fire under a flag of truce, he, too, was killed; that Bulgarian troops estimated at battalion strength with machine-guns and automatic weapons had then advanced and occupied positions on the ridges in Greek territory, endeavouring thereby to gain what advantage the ground offered. Furthermore, from 'information carefully collected on the part of authorized and competent authorities', it clearly appeared, according to this note, that the Bulgarians had by 'surprise and without provocation' opened fire. With 'premeditation' they had concentrated troops 'disproportionate' to those required under such circumstances. Though the Greeks had ceased fire, the Bulgarians had not, thereby killing the officer of the covering company.

The continued violation of Greek territory, the note observed, and its occupation by Bulgarian forces had been verified by reconnaissance. Thus orders had been issued to the 'military commander to repulse the invasion by taking all measures that he will judge *à propos* for the integrity of the national territory and its security, until satisfaction is given'. The demands that Hadjikyriakos had made to Dantcheff at their noon meeting were then repeated. In conclusion, the note maintained that, because of the 'gravity of the incident', the Athens government expected to receive from Sofia 'satisfaction with the least possible delay'.[6]

The next morning, 22 October, Dantcheff after receipt of the Greek note arranged an interview with Hadjikyriakos for noon. At this meeting the chargé reiterated the request for a cease-fire and transmitted the proposals of his government for the nomination of a mixed commission of inquiry. Dantcheff's proposals, however, were not accepted. The Foreign Minister maintained that inquiries were useless, given the incontestable responsibility falling on Bulgaria for the incident. Dantcheff, however, insisted a number of times to Hadjikyriakos on the necessity of preventing a simple frontier incident from degenerating into a serious conflict, as well as on the usefulness of delegating to a mixed commission of inquiry the task of establishing responsibility. He pointed out that in previous border incidents, many of them more serious, 'where the

[6] Text. Ibid., 25 Oct. 1925, p. 1.

responsibility of superior organs of Greek authority was gravely engaged', his government, 'instead of losing patience', had proffered the nomination of a mixed commission of inquiry; and that in these instances Sofia had proposed the nomination of two arbiters to fix, in common with Athens, the amount of the indemnity to be granted to the families of the slain Bulgarian soldiers. Hadjikyriakos was not moved by Dantcheff's pleadings and his formal refusal to accept any of the Bulgarian proposals compelled the chargé to request an immediate confrontation with the Prime Minister, General Pangalos, so he might present personally at the highest level the Bulgarian proposals and insist on their acceptance. The meeting was fixed for one o'clock.

In his half-hour meeting with Pangalos, Dantcheff was no more successful than he had been with Hadjikyriakos. Greek fears, real or imagined, of Bulgarian intentions had come to fruition. To the chargé's pleas Pangalos objected that Athens was in no position to accept them, 'as long as Bulgarian troops, belonging to the regular army and commanded by Bulgarian officers, trampled on Greek territory and continued the struggle'. Dantcheff observed that his government had 'affirmed categorically' that there was no Bulgarian advance into Greek territory and that the military had received 'strict orders to avoid all provocation' and not to reply to any Greek fire. Pangalos, however, was not persuaded by the chargé's words. There had been an invasion of Greek territory by Bulgarian forces and the Greek Government was unable to consent to a mixed commission of inquiry while the invasion continued. Dantcheff retorted that the very inquiry demanded by his government would establish in a 'positive and indubitable manner' the absence of any such invasion. Pangalos ignored the remark that the conditions stipulated by Athens removed all possibility of verifying the allegations of the Greek authorities as to a Bulgarian invasion. He instead requested that the chargé contact Sofia for a withdrawal of the Bulgarian troops from Greek territory, expressing the fear that the Commander of the Salonika Army Corps (the Third), forced to defend his area, may have 'already advanced his troops into Bulgarian territory' with the intention of forcing the invading Bulgars by a flanking movement to evacuate Greek territory. With these words the meeting terminated.[7] The interview had obviously got nowhere.

[7] Ministère des Affaires Étrangères (Bulgarie), Sur les démarches faites par le Chargé d'Affaires de Bulgarie à Athènes auprès du Gouvernement hellénique

Dantcheff's role, foredoomed before it began by events at the frontier and the Greek Ministry of War, had ended. Unknown to him, at six o'clock that morning Greek troops had entered Bulgarian territory via the Struma Valley.[8]

Advice for Moderation

Unaware of the Greek advance, Rosetti that same morning was contacted by Minkoff 'unofficially' by means of a 'personal communication'. The Secretary-General of the Bulgarian Foreign Ministry informed the chargé of the Greek action and relayed to him the information that the Bulgarian Army had orders to withdraw five kilometres from the frontier in order to avoid any collision with the oncoming Greek troops. As to the demands of the Athens government, which, telegraphed by Dantcheff, had now been received at the Foreign Ministry, Minkoff 'personally considered [them] very severe'.[9]

Arriving at the Bulgarian Foreign Ministry that morning, the British chargé d'affaires, Stevenson, found Minkoff in a state of extreme excitement. In talking to Stevenson 'his voice rarely fell below a loud shout'. He informed the British chargé of the withdrawal of Bulgarian garrisons from several frontier posts in the Struma Valley and of a Greek advance to a point four kilometres within the Bulgarian frontier. 'In stentorian tones and at the imminent risk of damages to his own fist and to the desk in front of him', Minkoff told Stevenson of the Greek reply to the repeated requests of his government for a joint inquiry. Athens, he felt, 'evidently thought that as Bulgaria was weak and defenceless she could treat her with impunity'. Indeed, General Pangalos had now made three demands, then, without waiting for a Bulgarian reply, had invaded. When it became possible for Stevenson to speak, he impressed on Minkoff that Bulgaria must avoid any act which might be interpreted as offensive, and strongly advised that no resistance be made to the Greek advance. Minkoff assured Stevenson that orders to that effect had been given to the Bulgarian forces at the frontier, and added that the Cabinet would probably decide later

au sujet de l'incident de frontière gréco-bulgare du Octobre 1925. Political 1925, League of Nations Archives.

[8] Report of the Commission of Enquiry into the Incidents on the Frontier between Bulgaria and Greece. Text. *Official Journal*, 7th year, 1926, p. 199.

[9] Rosetti (Sofia) to the F.Min., no. 1759, 22 Oct. 1925. Greek Archives.

that day to appeal to the League of Nations. In the interim, he continued, instructions had been dispatched to the Bulgarian Missions at London, Paris, and Rome to bring Sofia's case before the governments to which they were accredited, and to request their intervention with the Greek Government with a view to restraining it.

When Minkoff read the Greek note to Stevenson, the chargé had the impression from the tone of the note that it was not an ultimatum, but rather 'more of a proposal for negotiations', couched, he was willing to admit, in somewhat 'peremptory terms', but no more so than was usual in communications of this nature exchanged between Balkan states. This being so, he found it difficult to reconcile the Greek Government's attitude with that of the Greek military in Salonika, except by surmising a lack of co-ordination between the civil authorities in Athens and the military in Salonika, if not an actual attempt by the military to override the government. According to Bulgarian opinion, the Greek military had gained the upper hand, at least in Macedonia, and General Pangalos, faced with an extremely difficult internal situation, had acquiesced in the military action taken on the Bulgarian frontier in the hope that this would distract attention from home affairs.[10] As we have seen, Stevenson had already mentioned this notion to Rosetti, but the latter had rejected it. It was certainly entirely at variance with the way in which the Greek decision to invade Bulgaria had been taken.

Leaving the Bulgarian Foreign Ministry, Stevenson then called on Rosetti. He revealed to the Greek chargé that he had advised the Bulgarian Government to issue orders to its military not to oppose the Greek advance, so as to avoid a pitched battle. By doing so, the Bulgarians would place themselves in an 'advantageous position' *vis-à-vis* the Greeks in any subsequent settlement of the dispute. The Englishman also thought that in the afternoon the Bulgarian Government would appeal to the League of Nations to intervene and settle the dispute.[11]

Rosetti's own reactions were immediately telegraphed to Athens, following the dispatch of this message. Like Caftanzoglou, he, too, pleaded for moderation. He felt that since the Bulgars had already

[10] Stevenson (Sofia) to Chamberlain, no. 231, 28 Oct. 1925. File 13309, FO/371/10673, PRO.
[11] Rosetti (Sofia) to the F.Min., no. 1759, 22 Oct. 1925. Greek Archives.

been taught a lesson and the border areas reoccupied, it would be wise to stop the Greek advance and remain on the line retaken. Any further advance would perhaps weaken the Greek case and give the impression that another aim was being pursued: when provoked, Greece needed to occupy a portion of Bulgarian territory till she was given satisfaction.[12]

Rosetti was then visited by Lieutenant-Colonel Scanagatta, the Italian President of the Inter-Allied Military Organ of Liquidation, who was desirous of learning more about the Greek position. The colonel divulged that he had had an interview that morning with the Minister of War, Colonel Ivan Volkoff. The latter, according to Scanagatta, had been very 'uneasy' and had expressed his surprise at the events which had taken place. He was 'grieved' that the incident occurred during a period when Greek-Bulgarian relations appeared to have improved. He had then informed Scanagatta that he had given orders to the Bulgarian military to retreat without offering any resistance to the advancing Greeks. Scanagatta pointed out to the Greek chargé that, though the army would obey, he did not know what would be the 'position [of the] powerful Macedonian organizations' (i.e. the komitadjis), which the government in Sofia could not control. The Italian colonel feared that the Bulgars would ask the Allied Powers for increased military measures (i.e. mobilization). In an obvious reference to Article 66 of the Treaty of Neuilly, he pointed out that the Bulgarian Army was assigned to border security, but once that was violated, as the Greeks were violating it that very moment, the Bulgarian Government would be in a position to ask for increased military measures. Thus Scanagatta appeared to be saying that violation of the Bulgarian borders by the Greeks could perhaps justify a Bulgarian request for mobilization, though this was expressly forbidden under Article 68 of the Treaty of Neuilly. His own personal view was that the Greek invasion could perhaps provoke Yugoslav interference which in turn could produce 'other general complications'. Rosetti thought that the latter comment was an oblique hint of possible Italian intervention.[13]

---

[12] Rosetti (Sofia) to the F.Min., no. 1760, 22 Oct. 1925. Greek Archives.
[13] Rosetti (Sofia) to the F.Min., no. 1766, 22 Oct. 1925. Greek Archives.
Under Article 66 of the Treaty of Neuilly it was stipulated that the Bulgarian Army would be 'exclusively employed for the maintenance of order within Bulgarian territory and for the control of the frontiers'. On the other hand, under Article 68, 'all measures of mobilization or appertaining to mobilization are forbidden'.

Indeed, Colonel Scanagatta's fears of Yugoslav interference were not as far-fetched as would appear at first sight. His mistake, however, was to assume that Yugoslavia's hostility would be directed against Bulgaria, Italy's Balkan satellite, and that Sofia, because of its strained relations with Belgrade, would make no move to entice the latter capital into a combined action against Athens. On this very day, in fact, when asked by the British Minister in Belgrade, Sir Howard Kennard, what attitude his government would adopt in the present crisis, the Yugoslav Foreign Minister, Momčilo Ninčić, had replied that it 'would not tolerate any territorial changes in the region'. At the same time, he did not appear to display the eagerness to come to Athens's assistance that would have been natural in view of his professed readiness to support his Greek ally in case of necessity.[14] The Yugoslav's lack of eagerness was due to the fact that on the previous day, as he later admitted, the Bulgarian Government had requested Yugoslavia's intervention.[15] The Bulgarian proposal included an immediate military alliance, with a view to combined action against the Greeks, the joint spoils to be the port cities of Salonika, Kavala, and Alexandroupolis. After consideration of the offer, Ninčić rejected it[16] and declined to 'take any action which might be construed as giving either party support'.[17]

No sooner had Scanagatta departed than the Greek note, dispatched the previous night from Athens, arrived at the Greek Legation. Rosetti immediately hurried to the Foreign Ministry and presented a copy of the note, the contents of which were subsequently described by Sofia as *'quasi-ultimatifs'*,[18] to the Foreign

[14] Kennard (Belgrade) to Chamberlain, 22 Oct. 1925. File 13131, FO/371/10701, PRO; Belgrade to Athens, addressed to the F.O., no. 137, repeated to Sofia, 23 Oct. 1925. File 953, FO/286/916, PRO. See also Dodge (Belgrade) to the Dept. of State, 24 Oct. 1925. File 768.74/216, Record Group 59, NA; Dodge (Belgrade) to the Sec. of State, no. 2848, 24 Oct. 1925. File 768.74/231, Record Group 59, NA.

[15] Kennard (Belgrade) to Chamberlain, no. 409, 28 Oct. 1925. File 13309, FO/371/10673, PRO; Belgrade to Athens, addressed to the F.O., no. 137, repeated to Sofia, 23 Oct. 1925. File 953, FO/286/916, PRO.

[16] Erskine (Sofia) to Chamberlain, no. 240, 12 Nov. 1925. File 13309, FO/371/10673, PRO.

[17] Kennard (Belgrade) to Chamberlain, no. 409, 28 Oct. 1925. File 13309, FO/371/10673, PRO; Belgrade to Athens, addressed to the F.O., no. 137, repeated to Sofia, 23 Oct. 1925. File 953, FO/286/916, PRO.

[18] Ministère des Affaires Étrangères (Bulgarie), Récapitulation des événements concernant l'incident gréco-bulgare de Demir-Kapia jusqu'au moment de

Minister, Kristo D. Kalfoff. By this time it was 6.15 in the afternoon. It was Rosetti's first encounter with Kalfoff since the beginning of the incident. The latter expressed his 'sorrow' for what had
occurred and reassured the chargé that from the start his government had only wanted to settle the issue. However, he explained,
when no reply had been received from Athens to Sofia's proposals,
but on the contrary it was learned that the Greek Army was
advancing into Bulgarian territory on a front thirty kilometres wide,
had penetrated ten kilometres, and was bombarding Petrich, his
government had turned to the League of Nations, whose decisions
it would faithfully carry out. Since Petrich was an unfortified city,
Kalfoff begged that the Greek Government order a cessation of
fire.[19] On these words the interview ended.

While Rosetti was having these conversations, Stevenson was
consulting with the French Minister, Émile Dard, and the Italian
chargé d'affaires, Weill Schott Leone. Both of them completely
agreed with Stevenson to give the Bulgarians that afternoon 'more
or less similar advice'—to avoid provocative acts and not to resist
the Greek advance. Stevenson's own suggestion to London was that
Sir Milne Cheetham in Athens might use his influence with the
government 'in the direction of moderation'.[20] This was not the
first time that Stevenson, much to his credit ,would assume without
any instructions the initiative in solving this crisis.

The Italian chargé, believing that there were no obstacles involved in giving the Bulgarian Foreign Minister, Kalfoff, advice to
be 'calm [and] persuading him to defer [the] work [of] peace-
maker [to the] Great Powers', called at the Foreign Ministry. In
his interview with the Foreign Minister, as agreed, Leone advised

---

l'intervention du Conseil de la Société des Nations. Political 1925, League of
Nations Archives.
    The American chargé d'affaires, Philander L. Cable, thought that the press
had been in error in terming the Greek note an ultimatum. 'In reality', he felt it
was 'rather the working basis for an arrangement', although its terms were such
that the Greeks could scarcely have hoped for complete acceptance. (Cable
(Sofia) to the Dept. of State, 26 Oct. 1925. File 768.74/232, Record Group 59,
NA.)

    [19] Rosetti (Sofia) to the F.Min., no. 1767, 22 Oct. 1925. Greek Archives.
    [20] Sofia to Athens, addressed to the F.O., no. 78, and repeated to Belgrade
and Constantinople, 22 Oct. 1925. File 953, FO/286/916, PRO. See also Cable
(Sofia) to the Dept. of State, 26 Oct. 1925. File 768.74/232, Record Group 59,
NA.

calm. Kalfoff appeared to 'welcome the recommendation', assuring the chargé that his government would make every effort to keep the peace.[21]

Though the Italian chargé may have been successful with this type of advice in Sofia, the same could not be said for the British and French Ministers in Athens. That day, 22 October, Cheetham in the Greek capital informed the Foreign Office that the French Minister, Count Louis Charles Pineton de Chambrun, had tactfully warned the Secretary-General of the Greek Foreign Ministry, Caftanzoglou, of the 'danger of taking too strong a line with [the] Bulgarians'. Cheetham and Chambrun were both agreed, however, that at the present moment it would be impossible to approach the Prime Minister, General Pangalos, with any 'suggestions for settlement' of the affair. Pangalos, Cheetham felt, was 'almost forced by his anomalous position to pose as [the] energetic champion of Greek interests'. Accordingly, Cheetham thought that Pangalos would 'resent advice even if it could properly be offered'. It was difficult, he continued, as was the case with all these frontier flare-ups, to ascertain the facts and the real responsibility. The present situation, however, appeared, in the hands of the dictator, Pangalos, 'to be assuming more serious proportions than is usually the case'.[22]

Virtually demilitarized under the Treaty of Neuilly,[23] Bulgaria was really in no position to resist a Greek advance. Therefore, her first reaction was to make a general appeal and her second to ask for specific assistance. To her missions in Belgrade, Bucharest, London, Paris, and Rome, orders were issued requesting intervention with the government in Athens so that the military operations might be stopped. Bulgaria declared at the same time that she was prepared to submit the incident to investigation by an impartial commission of inquiry.[24]

---

[21] Weill Schott [Leone] (Sofia) to Mussolini, 22 Oct. 1925. Italian Archives.

[22] Athens to the F.O., no. 162, 22 Oct. 1925. File 953, FO/286/916, PRO.

[23] Under the Treaty of Neuilly, Part IV, Articles 64–104, Bulgaria had been stripped militarily and was impotent. Under Article 66 her army was not to exceed 20,000 men, while under Article 69 her gendarmes, customs officials, forest guards, and local or municipal police were not to exceed 10,000. In addition she could establish a special corps of frontier guards not exceeding 3,000 men. Therefore total rifles in Bulgaria were not to exceed 33,000.

[24] Ministère des Affaires Étrangères (Bulgarie), Récapitulation des événements concernant l'incident gréco-bulgare de Demir-Kapia jusqu'au moment de l'intervention du Conseil de la Société des Nations. Political 1925, League of Nations Archives.

As to specific assistance, Leone was asked personally by Kalfoff whether he would contact Italy's dictator, Benito Mussolini, to support a Bulgarian request that Rome intervene in Athens to stop the Greek advance. He was also asked whether Lieutenant-Colonel Scanagatta could go immediately to the invaded zone to verify events.[25] A similar proposal to authorize the sending of the French representative was made to Dard.[26]

That evening, Stevenson visited the Bulgarian Foreign Minister, Kalfoff, who had requested to speak to him. While he was waiting to see the Foreign Minister he again talked with Minkoff, 'who was still in a state of ungovernable excitement'. He informed Stevenson that Bulgaria had appealed to the League of Nations and observed that if all the people of Bulgaria rose and pushed the Greeks back into their own territory with nothing but their bare fists, no one would be able to deny them their right to do so. Moreover, Minkoff did not agree that such a course would be unwise. He thought that Bulgaria's appeal to the League in no way took away his country's right to defend itself.

The demeanour of the Foreign Minister on the other hand favourably surprised Stevenson. Kalfoff 'was obviously moved, but remained quite calm'. He also informed Stevenson of the Cabinet's decision to appeal to Geneva and assured him that the orders issued to the Bulgarian military, to retire as the Greeks advanced and not to resist, would be maintained, despite the fact that the Greeks were shelling the open town of Petrich and invading Bulgarian territory on a thirty-kilometre front to a depth of eight to ten kilometres.

He then informed Stevenson that Rosetti had delivered to him a note similar to that given to Dantcheff in Athens and explained that he had told Rosetti that, since the matter had been referred by the Bulgarian Government to the League of Nations, his government regretted their inability to negotiate the question directly with the Greek Government. The Bulgarian Foreign Minister then asked Stevenson to support his country's plea for intervention at Athens already made by the Bulgarian Legation in London and to request the British Government to authorize its representative on

---

[25] Weill Schott [Leone] (Sofia) to Mussolini, 22 Oct. 1925. Italian Archives.

[26] Ministère des Affaires Étrangères (Bulgarie), Récapitulation des événements concernant l'incident gréco-bulgare de Demir Kapia-jusqu'au moment de l'intervention du Conseil de la Société des Nations. Political 1925, League of Nations Archives; Weill Schott [Leone] (Sofia) to Mussolini, 23 Oct. 1925. Italian Archives.

the Inter-Allied Military Organ of Liquidation to proceed with his colleagues to the frontier to study the situation. He emphasized the necessity for speedy action and begged for a quick reply. Stevenson promised to communicate the request to London and then gave Kalfoff the same advice as he had already tendered to Minkoff—to take no offensive action and not to resist the Greek advance. The Foreign Minister thereupon promised Stevenson to give him due warning should his government decide to change its attitude. This could only happen, he explained, if the Greek Army committed excesses or advanced with the obvious intention of occupying a large area of the country and public opinion could not be restrained.

When Stevenson suggested that it was desirable to control the press in order to avoid exciting passions which it would not be easy to quell, and which might render the government's task in executing its policy of non-resistance more difficult, Kalfoff agreed. He said that the necessary steps to arrange this would be taken.

Stevenson noted to the Foreign Office that he was keeping in touch with his French and Italian colleagues. Rosetti, he noted, continued to urge moderation with the government in Athens, but without success. Indeed, Rosetti was of the opinion that a hint from Cheetham in Athens 'would be all that was necessary to restrain [the] Greek Government, and [was] extremely anxious that such a hint should be given'. The danger of the situation that the Greek advance had created was obvious. Petrich was the centre of Macedonian irredentism. The control of the whole district had long been in the hands of the Macedonian Revolutionary Organization. Moreover, Stevenson noted, many Bulgarian refugees from Greek Macedonia had settled in the area. The feeling of these refugees towards Greece was, at the best of times, the reverse of friendly. The effect upon these refugees of seeing those whose recent treatment of them had caused them to emigrate to Bulgaria now overrun their new homes in that country could be well imagined. Leaving aside the question of who was responsible, Stevenson considered 'if possible steps should not be taken to restrict [the] Greek incursion'.[27]

When the telegraphic version of this conversation reached

[27] Stevenson (Sofia) to Chamberlain, no. 231, 28 Oct. 1925. File 13309, FO/371/10673, PRO; Stevenson (Sofia) to the F.O., no. 79, 22 Oct. 1925. File 13309, FO/371/10672, PRO; Sofia to Athens, addressed to the F.O., no. 80, repeated to Belgrade and Constantinople, 22 Oct. 1925. File 953, FO/286/916, PRO.

London, Charles H. Bateman, in charge of Greek affairs for the Foreign Office's Central Department, minuted that the Bulgarian request that the British representative of the Inter-Allied Military Organ of Liquidation be instructed to go to the frontier to see what was occurring seemed to show that the Bulgars had a clean conscience. Indeed, apart from some initial confusion the case seemed very convincing against the Greeks. Whatever, Bateman continued, was the trouble's origin, the Greeks, who were on the right side, should have consented to an inquiry as requested by the Bulgarians 'instead of taking the law into their own hands'. He thought therefore that the best course would be to give instructions to Cheetham to inform the Greeks that whatever the initial cause of the trouble there could be 'no doubt that the further they go into Bulgaria the more they [were] prejudicing their case', which would be soon handled by the Council of the League of Nations. It was therefore in their best interests that Great Britain asked them to call a halt to their advance. As soon as Sofia called for an inquiry, Athens's refusal to meet the Bulgarians had put them in the wrong under the Covenant of the League of Nations and they were playing into the hands of the Bulgarians. The Greeks might also be reminded that, as parties to the Treaty of Neuilly which limited Bulgaria's armed forces, Great Britain could not 'stand by and watch Bulgaria being invaded and that should the [League] Council decide against Greece, we will not hesitate to take steps to enforce justice being done to Bulgaria'.[28]

Dispatching his last message for 22 October, Rosetti related the recommendations of the Allied representatives at the Bulgarian Foreign Ministry and made it clear to Athens that the decision of the Greek Government to advance into Bulgaria had 'caused [an] unfavourable impression' among these representatives. He therefore repeated his opinion that it would be wise to order a cease-fire so as not to alienate the support of the Great Powers who might 'come out diplomatically against us'. He also revealed that Kalfoff had reassured the British chargé, Stevenson, that Bulgaria would continue its passive attitude, but if the Greeks enlarged their present position it would reconsider that attitude. At any rate, Kalfoff promised to make no decisions without notifying the Allied representatives beforehand.[29] With the filing of this message

[28] Minute by C. H. Bateman, 23 Oct. 1925. File 13309, FO/371/10672, PRO.
[29] Rosetti (Sofia) to the F.Min., no. 1769, 22 Oct. 1925. Greek Archives.

Rosetti's busy day—not to mention Stevenson's—had come to an end. The Bulgarians, demilitarized, without allies, and therefore defenceless, had turned to the League of Nations—the one organization they felt could offer them succour.

Kalfoff's message to the Secretary-General of the League of Nations, Sir Eric Drummond, first sketched Sofia's version of the incident and then noted that Bulgarian proposals for a mixed commission to establish responsibilities for the incident had remained unanswered by Athens. On the contrary, Greek troops had advanced into Bulgarian territory, whose military had received orders not to resist. His appeal therefore protested 'with all possible vehemence against the flagrant invasion', by the army of a League member, of a country known to be disarmed. Thus, in virtue of Articles 10 and 11 of the Covenant of the League of Nations, Kalfoff requested that Drummond convene the League Council 'without delay to take the necessary steps'. Convinced that the Council would do its duty, Sofia, he concluded, would maintain its orders to the Bulgarian troops not to resist the Greek advance.[30] It was a promise that Kalfoff faithfully executed, but only, as we shall see, with the greatest difficulty.

[30] Text. League of Nations, *Official Journal*, 6th year, 1925, p. 1696.

III

COERCION: FIRST PHASE

Reactions in Geneva

THE Greek note and the subsequent advance into Bulgaria, as well as Kalfoff's appeal to Geneva, like a pebble thrown into a calm pool, had caused ripples of unease in cities and countries that had previously been untouched by these events.

The first city to manifest its anxieties was Geneva. On 21 October, while the Dantcheff-Hadjikyriakos discussions were taking place and the Greek note was being drafted in the Foreign Ministry, the Greek chargé d'affaires in Bern, Vassili Dendramis, was telegraphing to Athens that he had observed 'restlessness in League of Nations circles . . . regarding [the] Greek-Bulgarian border incident'. He requested therefore that the Foreign Ministry immediately communicate to him the 'dimensions' of the occurrence and whether the ministry foresaw any 'serious consequences'.[1]

That night, Dendramis was telephoned from Geneva by Arthur Salter, the English Director of the Economic and Financial Section of the League Secretariat, on orders from the Secretary-General, Sir Eric Drummond. This overture, it should be noted, was made well before Kalfoff's appeal to the League. According to Salter, information had reached the Secretariat via London that the Greek Government had handed the Bulgarians an 'ultimatum' demanding a reply within forty-eight hours. The Secretary-General, however, asked that Athens be informed that he had every conviction that Greece wanted to 'conform with [the] provisions [of the] Covenant [of the] League of Nations'.[2]

Athens's first reply was to the latter report and was dispatched on 22 October, the very day Greek forces crossed the Bulgarian frontier. It informed Dendramis that no ultimatum had been sent to Sofia, but only a diplomatic note, 'moderate' in tone, a copy of which had been forwarded to him.[3]

[1] Dendramis (Bern) to the F.Min., no. 3611, 21 Oct. 1925. Greek Archives.
[2] Dendramis (Bern) to the F.Min., no. 3618, 21 Oct. 1925. Greek Archives.
[3] Greek F.Min. to the Greek Legation in Bern, no. 14816, 22 Oct. 1925. Greek Archives.

In answer to Dendramis's first report, a second message was sent on 23 October, a full day after the advance into Bulgaria. The Greek Government, the chargé was curtly informed, hoped the border incident would have no serious repercussions, 'provided that Bulgaria accepts the terms of the diplomatic note delivered'.[4]

While these messages were heading towards Bern, Dendramis was urgently telegraphing Athens that the League's Secretary-General felt the 'greatest disquiet' over the incident. The French Director of the League's Political Section, Paul Mantoux, had telephoned to tell him that Council members and especially Sweden's representative, Foreign Minister Östen Undén, had telegraphed the Secretary-General asking for information, so that in case a threat or disturbance of the peace took place the Council would be in a position to take those 'measures dictated by the Covenant'.[5]

The following day, 23 October, at a time when Kalfoff's appeal had not yet reached Geneva, Dendramis was reporting that the prevailing opinion in the League Secretariat was that, if the incident were not solved by diplomatic means and if the Greek forces continued their advance to 'enforce by arms [the] terms [of the] diplomatic note' sent to Sofia, Bulgaria, or perhaps another power like Sweden, would act in order that the Council urgently undertake the question under Articles 11 and 15 of the Covenant. In that case it would undoubtedly decide to send to the frontier an investigation committee. Dendramis then emphasized to Athens the most serious consequences that would arise should any Greek actions be contrary to the provisions of Articles 10 and 12 of the Covenant. He also warned that Athens 'take into consideration [that] any invasion and occupation [of] Bulgarian territory without [a] previous appeal to [the] League of Nations will weaken [the] international position of Greece'. Should Greece ignore the League, she would place herself in opposition to all other League members. For the above reasons, the chargé opined, if the Bulgars refuse to satisfy Athens and if all means of settling the difference diplomatically are exhausted, then Greece should undertake the initiative and appeal to the League asking adjustment of the question on the basis of the terms proposed in Greece's note to Sofia.[6]

---

[4] Greek F.Min. to the Greek Legation in Bern, no. 14815, 23 Oct. 1925. Greek Archives.
[5] Dendramis (Bern) to the F.Min., no. 3621, 22 Oct. 1925. Greek Archives.
[6] Dendramis (Bern) to the F.Min., no. 3622, 23 Oct. 1925. Greek Archives.

The arrival of Kalfoff's appeal at Geneva prompted Dendramis urgently to contact Athens once again. If Athens desired, he telegraphed, to strengthen Greece's position before the League Council and to avoid all 'moral responsibility' for the incident falling on its shoulders and thus be found by the Council to have broken the Covenant, it was essential that the Greek Army withdraw immediately to the Greek frontier. The Greek representative would then be able to declare in any future Council debate that no Greek troops were to be found on Bulgarian territory.[7]

To strengthen his case in Athens, Dendramis telegraphed soon after that an 'English friend of ours, [a] higher official' of the League Secretariat, had recommended that the Greek Army withdraw from Bulgarian territory. Simultaneously, the Secretary-General was to be informed that the Greek Army, after re-occupying areas seized from the Bulgarian Army and safeguarding the national territory, had received orders to withdraw to Greek territory. The Secretary-General was also to be informed that the Greek Government would be represented at the next meeting of the League Council at Paris by a person to be soon designated. Only in this manner, Dendramis ended, could Greece's diplomatic position before the League Council be strengthened.[8]

Further impressions were reported by Dendramis soon after the dispatch of this last message. The League's Deputy Secretary-General, the Frenchman, Joseph Avenol, in a conversation with Thanassis Aghnides, a Greek national and a senior official in the League Secretariat's Political Section, had 'cautioned wisdom' to the Greek Government. Avenol noted that during the Corfu Incident two years before a great deal of sympathy had been shown for Greece. He stressed that many dangers encircled her which had to be taken into consideration. He thought that Athens must 'not think only for today but for tomorrow'. If a tragic event were to befall Greece the following day and resort were made to Geneva, it would be difficult for the League 'to move international public opinion' in her favour if in the present situation it could not show an adjustment of the Greek position 'towards [the] letter and the spirit [of the] Covenant of the League of Nations'.[9]

[7] Dendramis (Bern) to the F.Min., no. 3630, 23 Oct. 1925. Greek Archives.
[8] Dendramis (Bern) to the F.Min., no. 3646, 23 Oct. 1925. Greek Archives.
[9] Dendramis (Bern) to the F.Min., no. 3656, 23 Oct. 1925. Greek Archives.

Reactions in London, Paris, and Rome

Dendramis's advice, the anxieties of the Secretary-General, and the counsel of Avenol apparently made less of an impression on Athens than the words and admonitions of the Great Powers. During the first days, however, because of lags in communication, the Powers were put in the unenviable position of merely reacting to events that had already occurred in Athens and Sofia.

The next city after Geneva to show its concern was London. News of what had occurred at the frontier was supplied by Sir Milne Cheetham from Athens, who also informed the Foreign Office that, according to the Greek press, Athens had ordered a troop advance and the occupation of Petrich, as well as the dispatch of an ultimatum to Bulgaria demanding apologies and an indemnity. Cheetham, however, saw 'no reason at present to fear more serious complications'.[10] But the Foreign Office was uneasy.

Charles H. Bateman, in charge of Greek affairs for the Foreign Office's Central Department, minuted to Cheetham's message that no 'serious complications need arise' unless the Yugoslavs were a party to this incursion. The Foreign Office had much information leading them to believe that there was a move towards a Yugoslav-Bulgar rapprochement—possibly with the idea of bringing Athens to heel over the question of the renewal of the Yugoslav-Greek alliance. He hardly thought that the Yugoslavs would be associated with this sort of action. 'It is probably nothing more than a frontier incident', he concluded.[11] To this minute Charles Howard Smith, also of the Central Department, penned his agreement.[12] On the other hand, Miles W. Lampson, one of the Foreign Office's Counsellors and Head of the Central Department, was not so sure that it was merely another frontier incident. However, he noted, they could 'only wait and see'. There was nothing for the Foreign Office to do at the 'moment but watch developments'.[13] To this the Assistant Under-Secretary, Sir William Tyrrell, agreed.[14] By the next day, 22 October, Cheetham's dispatch and the above minutes

[10] Cheetham (Athens) to the F.O., no. 159, 21 Oct. 1925. File 13309, FO/371/10672, PRO.

[11] Minute by C. H. Bateman, 21 Oct. 1925. File 13309, FO/371/10672, PRO.

[12] Minute by C. Howard Smith, 21 Oct. 1925. File 13309, FO/371/10672, PRO.

[13] Minute by M. W. Lampson, 21 Oct. 1925. File 13309, FO/371/10672, PRO.

[14] Minute by Sir W. T., 21 Oct. 1925. File 13309, FO/371/10672, PRO.

were in the hands of the Foreign Secretary, Sir Austen Chamberlain, who wrote that the whole situation left him 'uneasy'.[15]

That same morning, with the Greek advance into Bulgaria yet unknown at the Foreign Office, Chamberlain was visited by the Swedish Minister, Baron Erik Kule Palmstierna. The minister had come to the Foreign Office on instructions from his government to express to Sir Austen the warmest congratulations of the Swedish Government and people for the success of the Locarno Conference. Chamberlain was gratified that the achievements of Locarno were as warmly approved of by other nations as by those directly involved.

On instructions, Palmstierna then asked Sir Austen his views on the Greek-Bulgarian 'quarrel' and whether he 'proposed to bring the matter before the Council of the League of Nations, especially in view of the news of an ultimatum by Greece'. Sir Austen replied that his 'information was at present too meagre' to enable him to 'take a decision'. Such information as he had had from Greece led him, 'however, to hope that the incident would not have dangerous results'.

Palmstierna then asked whether Sir Austen thought that Stockholm should take action. Chamberlain could not reply until he had fuller information, but for the moment he did not 'advise immediate reference to the League'. Closing the interview, the minister asked that he be kept informed of Sir Austen's views. Chamberlain promised that the Foreign Office would keep in touch with him.[16]

A similar view was expressed that day to the Italian Ambassador, Marchese Pietro Tomasi della Torretta, by the Assistant Under-Secretary of the Foreign Office, Sir William Tyrrell. Della Torretta, who had gone to the Foreign Office ostensibly to elicit information on the occurrences between Greece and Bulgaria, was told by Tyrrell that no news had arrived at the Foreign Office from Sofia and that the British Legation in Athens attached scant importance

---

[15] Minute by Sir A. C., 22 Oct. 1925. File 13309, FO/371/10672, PRO.

[16] Sir Austen Chamberlain to Sir Grant Duff (Stockholm), 22 Oct. 1925. File 13309, FO/371/10672, PRO; Chamberlain Papers.

The Swedish Minister and Stockholm's interest at the inception of the incident and throughout the course of its settlement can in large measure be explained by the actions of Sweden's Foreign Minister, Östen Undén, who played a very active role in League affairs during this period. Erik Lönnroth, 'Sweden: The Diplomacy of Östen Undén', in Gordon A. Craig and Felix Gilbert (eds.), The Diplomats 1919–1939 (Princeton University Press, 1953), pp. 86–99.

to the event, hinting in no way at an ultimatum and military measures. Sir William dismissed the frontier incident 'as one of the many that are in the habit of taking place in Balkan countries'. He added, however, that, if further information changed the picture, 'he would propose to Chamberlain to enter into relation[s] immediately with the Cabinets [of] Rome and Paris in order to proceed to [an] exchange of ideas'.[17] This, as we shall see, was the procedure adopted.

It was probably soon after these interviews that the news of what had actually happened between Athens and Sofia was received from Cheetham.[18] The arrival of this disturbing information was soon followed by a visit from the Greek Minister, Caclamanos, who called on Howard Smith at the Central Department.

He started the interview with a Greek version of the incident, and maintained that the Greek note to the Bulgars was not an ultimatum. Caclamanos then admitted that he had received no instructions from Athens to make representations to the British Government and that the whole 'question disturbed him very much'. First, as the Athens government was a purely military one, and since Hadjikyriakos had replaced Rentis at the Foreign Ministry, 'moderate counsels [were] less likely to prevail in Athens'. There was no doubt that considerable popular excitement existed in Athens because of the Bulgarian disregard of the white flag carried by the Greek officer who was killed. It likewise appeared significant to Caclamanos that the Bulgarians had chosen this moment for an attack, seeing that in ten days' time the Greek-Yugoslav Treaty of Alliance automatically lapsed. Moreover, he asked, why should the Bulgars choose to attack at a point which was so close to the Yugoslavian frontier? For all these reasons the Greek Minister was nervous that there was really more to the affair than a mere frontier incident. He was apprehensive lest the incident 'reach larger proportions'. Caclamanos then said that he had heard that the Bulgars had asked the Inter-Allied Military Organ of Liquidation at Sofia for permission to mobilize—a possible Bulgar move mentioned by Colonel Scanagatta to Rosetti and prohibited, as we have seen, by the Treaty of Neuilly. To all these remarks Howard Smith made no comment. He promised, however, to pass

---

[17] Torretta (London) to Mussolini, 23 Oct. 1925. Italian Archives.
[18] Cheetham (Athens) to the F.O., no. 164, 22 Oct. 1925. File 13309, FO/371/10672, PRO.

on Caclamanos's remarks and he 'sincerely trusted that what appeared to be a small frontier incident would not be allowed to become a really serious matter'.[19]

The Greek Minister was soon followed to the Foreign Office by the Bulgarian Minister, Pontcho Hadji Misheff, who likewise had an interview with Howard Smith. Unlike Caclamanos, however, Misheff was calling because of instructions that he had received from his government. He gave, as one would have expected, the Bulgarian version of the incident and recalled Sofia's proposals to Athens to investigate the affair jointly. Sofia had now heard that the Greek Army was advancing into Bulgarian territory and was bombarding Petrich. Misheff then observed cynically that the Greek advance was somewhat rapid work considering that this had been nothing more than a small border incident, that Bulgaria had immediately said that she was prepared to have the incident impartially examined and that if the Greeks found a Greek-Bulgar investigatory commission unacceptable, it could be investigated under the auspices of the League or by the addition to the commission of neutral members. Misheff assured Howard Smith that his government had no 'intention of making this a real quarrel'. He explained that he had been instructed to ask whether Chamberlain 'could not make friendly representations at Athens counselling moderation'. He therefore asked Howard Smith to convey his proposal and wanted to know whether the British Government would accept it, so that he could communicate as quickly as possible with Sofia.[20]

Caclamanos by his call to the Foreign Office had attempted to forestall the effect of any Bulgarian communication to the British Government. In his report to Athens he explained that his statement on the incident had been extracted from Greece's note addressed to Sofia the previous day. It was Caclamanos's impression that official British circles 'recognized the responsibility' of Bulgaria for what had occurred and even the 'justification' of the 'decision to remove from the national territory these violators'— comments in no way justified by his interview with Howard Smith, but which were intended to ingratiate him with the military government in Athens. This statement would make more acceptable and palatable to the military in Athens his next comment, namely, that

[19] Minute by Howard Smith, 22 Oct. 1925. File 13309, FO/371/10672, PRO.
[20] Minute by Howard Smith, 22 Oct. 1925. File 13309, FO/371/10672, PRO.

Greece's military action had raised the fear that complications might arise, and there was agitation that the peace was being jeopardized—comments reflecting Caclamanos's and Howard Smith's apprehensions. Furthermore, he feared that the Bulgars had deemed the moment opportune and the situation in the Balkans uneasy, and had initiated their attack on the Greek frontier at a point near the Yugoslav border with the hope that complications would arise from which they might benefit. This fear, he added parenthetically, was not exclusively his. The minister reminded Athens that the internal Bulgarian situation was 'not at all pleasant'. All these facts, he was sure, had not escaped the attention of the British Government. In London, it was generally thought that the solution of the incident might be to 'bring [the] friendly intervention [of the] League of Nations', an opinion echoed by the evening newspapers.

Shortly after his departure from the Foreign Office, Caclamanos continued, he was followed by the Bulgarian Minister, who, as expected, gave the Bulgarian version of what had occurred during the preceding days. The minister added that the British chargé d'affaires in Sofia had informed the Foreign Office that the Bulgars had proposed a commission of inquiry, but no reply had been received from Athens. Lastly, he noted, newspaper correspondents in Sofia were maintaining that the Bulgarian Government would appeal to the League and that, in order to protect its territory, permission to mobilize had been asked from the Allied Powers.[21]

By the time Caclamanos sent this report to Athens, the Foreign Office's decision on the handling of the affair had crystallized, and the appropriate instructions to co-ordinate Great Power action in both Athens and Sofia—which Tyrrell had told the Italian Ambassador he would propose to Chamberlain if the situation deteriorated—had been urgently dispatched to Paris and Rome. The British Ambassadors in both of these capitals were informed of the visits to the Foreign Office of the Greek and Bulgarian Ministers, who had given their versions of what had transpired. As was to be expected, the two versions in no way coincided as to who was responsible for what had occurred. Leaving responsibility aside, 'the question of the moment', according to the Foreign Office, was 'to prevent what was apparently a frontier incident from developing

---

[21] Caclamanos (London) to the F.Min. no., 2816, 22 Oct. 1925. Greek Archives.

into definite hostilities'. Each ambassador was therefore instructed to approach immediately the Foreign Minister of the country to which he was accredited and relate to him the gist of Stevenson's telegram of the previous day, calling the Foreign Minister's attention to the Bulgarians' apparent readiness to accept a joint Greek-Bulgar investigatory commission, a proposal to which the Greeks so far had not responded. Moreover, it was suggested that instructions should be communicated at once to the Italian and French Ministers at Athens and Sofia to consult with their British colleagues. They were to offer immediately 'counsels of moderation' to both states and to urge the calling of an immediate truce 'in order that an inquiry may be held and time given for passions to cool'.

Because the matter was most urgent, the Foreign Office was repeating these instructions to the legations in Athens and Sofia and was authorizing its ministers at these missions, 'should they think [the] matter brooks of no delay to deal with it at once at their own discretion', keeping, of course, at the same time in the closest touch with their Italian and French colleagues. If, however, this intervention was to 'prove ineffective, there always remain[ed] [the] machinery of the League to be invoked', the instructions concluded.[22]

During these days the French Minister in Athens, Chambrun, had shared with the French Foreign Minister, Aristide Briand, his fears about the situation that was developing.[23] It is probably safe to suppose that reports similar to Chambrun's were also sent to the Quai d'Orsay by the French Minister in Sofia, Dard. Thus when Lord Crewe, the British Ambassador in Paris, as instructed by the Foreign Office, saw Briand on the afternoon of 23 October and gave him the sense of Stevenson's communication describing what had transpired between Sofia and Athens, Briand explained to Crewe that on the previous night and again that very morning he had communicated to the French Ministers in Athens and Sofia instructing them to act in concert with their British colleagues. They had also been instructed to call on the two governments to suspend their actions, in view of the proposed meeting of the League Council scheduled to convene in Paris. Furthermore

---

[22] F.O. to Athens, no. 124, addressed to Paris and Rome, repeated for Sofia, 22 Oct. 1925. File 953, FO/286/916, PRO.

[23] Count Louis Charles Pineton de Chambrun, *Traditions et souvenirs* (Flammarion, 1952), p. 93.

they were to warn both the Bulgars and the Greeks with the utmost severity of the heavy responsibility in the eyes of the League that would fall upon the country that 'continued hostile action against its neighbour'. Evidently, Lord Crewe observed, Briand was confident that this reminder to both Athens and Sofia would be effective.[24] As Chambrun subsequently wrote with some liberty, Briand's instructions were: 'Arrière les fusils, arrière les mitrailleuses!'[25]

The same day, the French Ambassador in London, Aimé de Fleuriau, called at the Foreign Office on instructions from Briand. It was the latter's opinion, he informed John D. Gregory, one of the Foreign Office's Counsellors and Head of the Northern Department, that the border incident, regardless of who was responsible, required 'immediate and energetic action' in the Greek and Bulgarian capitals by Great Britain, France, and Italy 'with a view to stopping [the] hostilities and having the dispute referred to the League of Nations'. In addition, it was Briand's request that London convey urgent instructions to its missions in Athens and Sofia to act in this way. It was obvious from the content of the French Ambassador's remarks that his instructions from Paris had crossed with the instructions that had been conveyed by the Foreign Office to Lord Crewe the previous day and which had been presented by him to Briand that very afternoon. Almost instinctively Chamberlain in London and Briand in Paris had simultaneously thought along the same lines: to co-ordinate Great Power action in the two Balkan capitals. The French Foreign Minister, however, unlike Chamberlain, had gone one step further, in that he hoped to have the dispute referred to the League.

Fleuriau then pointed out to Gregory that the French Minister in Athens had already been instructed to say that the Greek Government's attitude 'was such as to arouse grave suspicions and that it appeared to be taking action out of all proportion to the incident'. Conversely, the Bulgarians were being advised to neglect nothing which could legitimately give the Greeks satisfaction.

Gregory observed that though Fleuriau's instructions from Briand were not completely identical with those already sent to Lord Crewe, he proposed to inform Fleuriau, who was returning the following morning to learn of any later developments, that events had moved so quickly that any further instructions to the two Balkan capitals 'would be superfluous and out of date'. To this note from Gregory, Chamberlain minuted that the British Ministers in Athens and Sofia should support any representations along these lines, and he supposed they would do so 'without further instructions'.[26]

Fleuriau, however, returned to the Foreign Office later that day and again called on Gregory. He informed Gregory that Sofia had requested that the French representative on the Inter-Allied Military Organ of Liquidation be authorized to proceed to the frontier to verify the facts. Briand, it was explained to Gregory, had refused Sofia's request. He did so on the grounds that it was better to leave to the League of Nations, already aware of the affair, the task of investigating it, and 'that in any case it was desirable to give it an international character'.[27]

While these exchanges were going on between London and Paris, the French Ambassador in Rome, René Besnard, appeared at the Italian Foreign Ministry. The purpose of his visit was to discuss with the Secretary-General of the Ministry, Salvatore Contarini, Italian participation in the projected measures to co-ordinate the actions of the Powers in Athens and Sofia.[28] In Paris, however, these measures of co-ordination were being slightly altered by unexpected events. Briand, in a conversation with the Italian Ambassador, Baron Camillo Romano Avezzana, related the steps being taken in Rome and London on the part of the French Government towards a settlement of the dispute. At the same time Avezzana was informed by Briand that, as Acting President of the League Council, he might have to convene the Council at Paris for that coming Monday, 26 October, 'for the purpose of taking measures on the case'.[29] It would therefore appear that even *before* the arrival of Kalfoff's appeal to the League, Briand was thinking of convening the League Council to handle the question.[30] Hence, the arrival of

[26] A note by J.D.G., 23 Oct. 1925, and attached minute by Sir A.C., 23 Oct. 1925. File 13309, FO/371/10672, PRO.

[27] Minute by J.D.G., 23 Oct. 1925. File 13309, FO/371/10672, PRO.

[28] Letter from the French Ambassador in Rome, René Besnard, to the Secretary-General of the Royal Italian Ministry of Foreign Affairs, Salvatore Contarini, dated 23 Oct. 1925. Italian Archives.

[29] Romano [Avezzana] (Paris) to Mussolini, 23 Oct. 1925. Italian Archives.

[30] In a conversation with the first secretary of the Greek Legation, Léon Melas, on the afternoon of 23 October it was admitted by two senior officials of

the Bulgarian appeal at the League's headquarters in Geneva later that day to request a convention of the Council seems to have coincided with Briand's own unannounced desires.

Briand's message to the Greek and Bulgarian Governments was short and to the point. The Secretary-General of the League of Nations, he informed them, acting under Article 11, had convened a special session of the League Council for Monday, 26 October, at Paris. The question would be examined during that meeting, with Bulgarian and Greek representatives present. In the meantime he reminded both Athens and Sofia of their solemn obligations as League Members under Article 12 of the Covenant, not to resort to war and the 'grave consequences which [the] Covenant lays down for breaches thereof'. Thus he exhorted both governments to give immediate orders that, pending examination of the dispute by the League Council, 'not only no further movements shall be undertaken, but that troops shall at once retire behind their respective frontiers'.[31]

With the League now actively involved in the whole question, it was necessary to alter slightly the instructions sent to the French Ambassador, Besnard, in Rome. The new orders imparted by the Quai d'Orsay were that Besnard was to ask the Italian Government that its ministers at Athens and Sofia intervene collectively with their French and British colleagues in order 'to put an immediate end to the hostilities and to entrust to the League of Nations the settlement of the conflict'. Besnard explained to the Secretary-General, Contarini, that, though the Bulgars had asked that the French representative on the Inter-Allied Military Organ of Liquidation be sent to the invaded area to verify the facts, his government had decided against it. The French Government, according to Besnard, considered it preferable to entrust to the League any inquiry it might deem useful.

He further revealed that from information he had received it appeared that the Bulgarian Government would not send any reinforcements to the frontier until it had received replies from the Powers and the League of Nations. The French Minister in Sofia,

---

the Quai d'Orsay that 'l'initiative de M. Briand a été prise avant' the Bulgarian Government had brought the question to the League of Nations. Carapanos to the F.Min., no. 4814, 23 Oct. 1925. French Text. Greek Archives.

[31] Text. League of Nations, *Official Journal*, 6th year, 1925, pp. 1696–7.

however, feared that the Bulgarian military might not conform with these orders.[32]

Besnard's overtures were not relayed by Mussolini to the Italian Missions until the following day, 24 October. According to the Duce, the formula proposed by the French Ambassador was in line with instructions already issued by the Italian Foreign Ministry and therefore acceptable. Because of the French decision declining to send their representative on the Inter-Allied Military Organ of Liquidation into the invaded zone, and Mussolini's undoubted desire to co-ordinate policies, the Italian chargé in Sofia was informed that the Bulgarian request to send Colonel Scanagatta to the invaded zone did not appear useful and would, in fact, be harmful.[33] Thus the Great Powers, after a momentary delay, began to co-ordinate their policies, which because of similar interests fortuitously coincided. As Della Torretta subsequently and succinctly expressed it to the Foreign Office, he was satisfied, 'by [the] identity of views and action existing between the Cabinets [of] London and Rome' on this question[34]—and, he might also have added, Paris.

The League Council is Convened

Soon after Briand, as Acting President of the League Council, had sent his message to the Greek and Bulgarian Governments, as well as new instructions to Besnard in Rome, he summoned the Greek Minister in Paris, Alexandros Carapanos, to the Quai d'Orsay. When Carapanos arrived, Briand recommended that in the interests of both countries 'hostilities cease in the zone of conflict', orders having been given to the Bulgarians to withdraw their troops from Greek territory. He stressed the profound impression caused by the bombardment of Petrich, which, according to news he had received from London, had greatly moved the Foreign Office and the British public. In response, Carapanos emphasized the declarations of 'pacific intentions' of his government, but added that he would transmit Briand's recommendations to Athens, and reply to him accordingly. Closing the interview, Briand inquired who would be

[32] Letter from the French Ambassador in Rome, René Besnard, to the Secretary-General of the Royal Italian Ministry of Foreign Affairs, Salvatore Contarini, dated 23 Oct. 1925. Italian Archives.

[33] Mussolini to Athens, Belgrade, London, Paris, and Sofia Missions, 24 Oct. 1925. Italian Archives.

[34] Torretta (London) to Mussolini, 25 Oct. 1925. Italian Archives.

designated to represent Greece at the Monday meeting of the League Council called to handle the frontier incident. Since Carapanos was in no position to answer, he turned to Athens for instructions.[35]

Later that day, Carapanos charged the first secretary of the Greek Legation, Léon Melas, to communicate to the Director of Political Affairs, Jules Laroche, and to the Director of Balkan Affairs, Charles Corbin, a note from the Greek Foreign Ministry explaining the reasons for the Greek advance.[36] Melas was to explain the situation arising from the Bulgarian attack and to stress the peaceful intentions of his government. In the discussion that followed at the Foreign Ministry, Laroche and Corbin did not conceal from Melas the 'preoccupation and the uneasiness caused to the French Government [by the] alarming situation provoked by the frontier incident which could involve very serious consequences'. They stated that 'instead of recourse to pacific means for settlement of the incident, the Greek Government had [had] recourse to force'. Such procedures were surprising 'on the morrow of the Locarno Conference which had affirmed the pacific desire of the West'. Thus the French Government, faithful to its policy, followed the development of events with the greatest attention. 'Deeply interested' in maintaining the peace and desiring to prevent an armed clash between Greece and Bulgaria, the Quai d'Orsay had 'immediately arranged a common plan of action with the British and Italian Governments in order that they charge their representatives at Athens to support the *démarche*' issued to the French Minister at Athens. In Paris, it was explained to Melas, Briand had taken the initiative and immediately convened the League Council which would meet there that coming Monday. This action of the French Foreign Minister had been taken *before* the Bulgarian Government's appeal had brought the question to the League of Nations.

[35] Carapanos (Paris) to the F.Min., no. 3832, 23 Oct. 1925. French Text. Greek Archives.

[36] In a circular note to all Greek Missions, the Foreign Ministry explained that the continuing Bulgarian occupation of Greek territory had forced the Greek Army to thrust towards Petrich, skirting the Bulgarian line, thus forcing the Bulgars to retire from Greek soil. This was done to avoid a frontal assault and unnecessary loss of life. The Greek Army had also been given strict orders to make no further advance as long as the Bulgars did not undertake fresh operations. The missions were asked to deliver the message to the Foreign Minister of the host country and to give it the widest circulation. Greek F.Min. to all Greek Missions, no. 14874, 22 Oct. 1925. Greek Archives.

Carapanos observed to Athens that considering what had been told to Melas, and despite the assurances of the Greek Government, the attitude of the French Government remained 'unfavourable to us'.[37]

A similar atmosphere, of course, also prevailed in London. When Caclamanos appeared at the Foreign Office that morning, 23 October, to deliver the Greek note explaining the reasons for the Greek advance—as Melas had done in Paris—he was seen by Miles W. Lampson, one of the Foreign Office's Counsellors and Head of the Central Department. It was for Caclamanos an uncomfortable interview. Lampson expressed himself in 'general as being astonished' that Athens 'could have been so foolish as to allow this frontier incident to degenerate into what threatened to become an international conflict of first-class dimensions. Lampson told Caclamanos that he would speak to him with the greatest frankness. He could not understand how the Athens government had failed to perceive the terrible consequences of their action. Leaving aside the graver issues, the mere chance of hostilities with Sofia would shatter Greece's credit. It was all very sad. By their action the Greeks might well have set fire to the Balkans. Caclamanos replied that he was sure that this had been a *coup* prepared by the Bulgarians. It was clear that the attack had been premeditated and the incident prepared long ago. He believed, therefore, that it was a trap. To this Lampson replied that, in that case, he was really in no position to congratulate the Greek Government on the action that they had taken. It appeared to him that the Greeks had walked into the Bulgarian trap—assuming for argument's sake that such a trap had indeed been set. For himself, Lampson failed to understand why the Bulgars should have set such a trap. What conceivable gain could the Bulgarians derive from it—disarmed as they were? On the other hand, Greece, whose relations with Yugoslavia as everyone knew were at that moment 'somewhat precarious'— here Lampson was undoubtedly alluding to the strained negotiations over the Salonika-Ghevgheli railway line which the Yugoslavs wished to be administered by a joint Yugoslav-Greek-French company, and the suspended negotiations for the renewal of the Greek-Yugoslav Treaty of Alliance—had, it appeared, 'deliberately provoked or embarked upon hostilities' with the Bulgars, regardless

[37] My italics. Carapanos to the F.Min., no. 4814, 22 Oct. 1925. French Text. Greek Archives.

of the danger that this entailed for the peace of the Balkans and especially for herself. Here Lampson informed the Greek Minister that the Foreign Office had heard from Stevenson in Sofia that the Bulgarians had announced to the Greeks their readiness to have an inquiry held on the affair. As far as the Foreign Office's information went, no response to this Bulgarian offer had been made by Athens. Caclamanos would forgive him saying so, Lampson continued, but Athens's silence had not made a favourable impression on the Foreign Office. This was not the moment to get involved in details. According to Lampson the most important thing was to prevent the border conflict from spreading. He then divulged to Caclamanos the gist of the instructions sent to Athens and Sofia the previous night. He read him extracts from the instructions and begged Caclamanos to reinforce these instructions by himself communicating with the government in Athens. Lampson added that since these instructions had been dispatched there had been a further development, for he had just heard that a special meeting of the League Council had been convened for Paris in the coming week to deal with the question. As a personal observation, Lampson added that it had occurred to him that Athens would have been better advised to have suggested the League appeal itself than to have resorted to actions which amounted to hostilities, thus leaving it open to the other side to initiate an appeal to the League.

Caclamanos replied to all this that he would immediately contact Athens, giving them the gist of Lampson's observations. The Greek Minister now wanted to state his own view, which was that, if the Bulgars would order the evacuation of such Greek territory as was now under their control, it was 'very probable' that the Athens government, on their side, would order the Greek troops to evacuate the Bulgarian territory they now held, in which case the atmosphere would be greatly improved by the time the League Council came to consider the question in Paris. Lampson replied that he would take note of what Caclamanos had said. Though he had said it was merely his personal opinion, Lampson urged the Greek Minister to embody that personal opinion in a communication to the Athens government, who would in turn perhaps be willing to assume the initiative and evacuate the territory they controlled without waiting for the Bulgarians to move first.[38]

[38] Memorandum of a Conversation between Mr. M. W. Lampson and M. Caclamanos, 23 Oct. 1925. File 13309, FO/371/10672, PRO.

When he had read the record of this conversation, Chamberlain minuted that he approved of 'Mr. Lampson's language' to the Greek Minister.[39] Howard Smith noted that according to the latest information supplied by Reuter's news agency, the Greeks had stopped their advance into Bulgaria, and it was therefore to be hoped that hostilities on the frontier would cease. At the same time, Howard Smith thought it might be useful for the League Council to have a report on the situation from the Allied military observers at Sofia.[40] The Assistant Under-Secretary, Tyrrell, doubted the 'wisdom' of this suggestion, first, because the matter was in the Council's hands, and second, because he fancied 'the idea would not be welcome to the Greeks'. He thought the Foreign Office might, for the moment, let the idea rest.[41]

Caclamanos's visit, however, was communicated to Cheetham in Athens. The impression left in the Foreign Office after the conversation that Caclamanos had had with Lampson was that the Greek Minister 'was distinctly nervous' as a result of the appeal to the League Council, and hoped by some means to get the incident on the way towards a settlement before the Council convened. There was no need to repeat that if Cheetham could properly do anything to assist in such a settlement, he had the Foreign Secretary's 'full authority to do so'. Cheetham was, of course, to remain in closest contact with his French and Italian colleagues.[42]

Caclamanos's visit was soon followed by one from the Bulgarian Minister, Misheff, who also, like Caclamanos, was received by Lampson. Misheff began the interview by reading a series of messages that he had received from Sofia. These were explanations of the endeavours that the Bulgarian Government had made to settle the dispute peacefully by arrangement with the Greek Government—its three proposals through Rosetti, and Dantcheff in Athens, that a mixed inquiry should be held with the purpose of ascertaining the blame for the incident. These overtures had received no reply, Misheff explained, although the Bulgarians had pointed out to the Greeks that the procedure proposed was well adapted for the settlement of the question in a manner consonant with normal friendly relations between neighbouring states. Faced

---

[39] Minute by Sir A.C., 23 Oct. 1925. File 13309, FO/371/10672, PRO.
[40] Minute by Howard Smith, 23 Oct. 1925. File 13309, FO/371/10672, PRO.
[41] Minute by Sir W.T., 23 Oct. 1925. File 13309, FO/371/10672, PRO.
[42] F.O. to Athens, no. 128, 23 Oct. 1925. File 953, FO/286/916, PRO.

with mere silence from Athens on the proposals, the Bulgarian Government had been forced to appeal to the League, invoking Articles 10 and 11 of the Covenant.

Misheff then recounted the depth of the Greek invasion and the orders issued to the Bulgarian forces to offer no resistance to this advance. The Bulgarians denied categorically that they had occupied any Greek territory. Finally Sofia had suggested to the British, French, and Italian Legations that their representatives on the Inter-Allied Military Organ of Liquidation should proceed to the frontier and verify what was occurring there for themselves.

Lampson's response to all this was to inform Misheff of the instructions that had already been sent to Athens and Sofia, and to read to the Bulgarian Minister the pertinent extracts from these instructions. He added that he had made a similar communication to Caclamanos that morning and had begged the Greek Minister to reinforce the Foreign Office's representations to the Athens government. Lampson then asked Misheff to do the same with his government. This Misheff promised to do at once.

Lampson then observed that if, in the interim that must elapse before any League action was possible, any friendly overtures should reach Sofia from Athens, the Foreign Office naturally hoped that the Bulgarian Government would receive these overtures in a conciliatory spirit. He did not know if any such overtures would be made or not, but if the Greeks did make them and if they were acted upon, it seemed to Lampson just possible that by the time the League machinery began to move, the present situation between Bulgaria and Greece might conceivably have improved to some degree, which naturally would make the Council's task much easier.

Misheff replied that it was very difficult to see what more Sofia could do. There were strict orders to the military not to resist and they had made three attempts at conciliation with Athens, to which there had been no reply. The Bulgarian Minister did not see that they could make any more useful overtures. Lampson saw that this might be so, but there was the possibility that Athens might see the light and make some attempt to contact Sofia. If Athens did contact Sofia, the Foreign Office hoped that Misheff's government would not rebuff the Greek attempt. Misheff said he would note this and communicate it to Sofia accordingly.[43] As in his interview with

[43] Memorandum of a Conversation between Mr. M. W. Lampson and M. Misheff, 23 Oct. 1925. File 13309, FO/371/10672, PRO.

Caclamanos, the language used by Lampson was approved by Chamberlain.[44]

In his communication to Athens, Caclamanos explained that the instructions sent to the British representatives at Athens and Sofia ordered them to take urgent steps with both governments, advising 'moderation' and recommending an immediate agreement for a cessation of hostilities. These steps, the Foreign Office had explained to him, would give time for passions to cool and an impartial investigation of the incident to take place. He was further told that a peaceful arrangement of the question coincided 'not only with the desire of the Powers' but also with the interests of Greece. According to the Foreign Office, the Bulgarian Government would be advised to order the immediate evacuation of its troops from Greek territory as one of the important preconditions to calming the situation.[45] He was informed at the Foreign Office that the British Government, desiring to prevent a simple frontier incident from degenerating into serious hostilities, had asked Paris and Rome that their representatives 'intervene at Athens and Sofia in the same sense as the English representative[s]'.[46]

[44] Minute by Sir A.C., 23 Oct. 1925. File 13309, FO/371/10672, PRO.

[45] Caclamanos (London) to the F.Min., no. 2826, 23 Oct. 1925. Greek Archives.

[46] Caclamanos (London) to the F.Min., no. 2828, 23 Oct. 1925. French Text. Greek Archives.

Writing in March of 1937, on the death of Sir Austen Chamberlain, Caclamanos in a letter to *The Times* reminisced about what had occurred twelve years before. According to Caclamanos, in an interview with Sir Austen, he had attempted to explain what had induced the actions of his government; the Foreign Secretary, however, had refused to express any opinion on the facts presented to him. Sir Austen replied to Caclamanos that he was sure the Bulgarian Minister would certainly relate a very different story. 'He wanted, however, as an old friend of Greece and the British statesman responsible for the conduct of . . . British foreign policy', to give, through Caclamanos, to the Athens government 'the most urgent advice' to withdraw its troops from Bulgaria and to end the incident as quickly as possible. Greece, Chamberlain noted, was surrounded by 'rivals rather than friends, and her disinterested friends and protectors were too far from the spot to give an effective support'.

Caclamanos then wrote that he gave an extensive summary of the conversation to the Greek Foreign Ministry, 'insisting on the great importance of the grave warning given by the British Foreign Secretary'. He felt that his government, on the basis of this telegram, decided immediately to settle matters by withdrawing its troops, the Bulgarians being advised to avoid any moves which could be considered provocative. Subsequent League action, the former Greek Minister wrote, was 'a mere procedure of ratification of what Sir Austen Chamberlain had obtained by his influence as British Foreign Secretary'. *The Times* (London), 19 March, 1937, p. 18.

The other news that Caclamanos sent to Athens that day must have emphasized to General Pangalos and Admiral Hadjikyriakos the deep concern over the whole question felt by the British Government and especially the Foreign Office: this was the news that Sir Austen Chamberlain, the Foreign Secretary himself, would go in person to the forthcoming Council session at Paris as Great Britain's representative.[47]

What Caclamanos did not report, for he may not have been aware of it, was that the decision to send Chamberlain to the League Council meeting had been made at a sitting of the British Cabinet that same day. Chamberlain had explained to his Cabinet colleagues the approaches that the Greeks and the Bulgars had made to the Foreign Office. Both had, however, given contradictory accounts of what had occurred. Until the previous day, reports reaching the Foreign Office had led Chamberlain to hope that the incident would not prove serious. That morning, however, he had heard of the Bulgarian appeal to the League, and of Briand's summoning of a Council meeting which Chamberlain felt as Foreign Secretary he was 'bound to attend'. His Cabinet colleagues, conscious of the strain which this would place on Chamberlain 'so soon after his return from his arduous labours at Locarno', nevertheless recognized the desirability of his attending the forthcoming Council meeting, and accordingly gave their assent. [48]

The advantage to be gained by the attendance of the British Foreign Secretary at any League meeting on this question had not escaped the attention of the League Secretary-General, Sir Eric Drummond. Accordingly Drummond had that day, 23 October, communicated very urgently to the Foreign Office via the British Consul at Geneva, asking that Chamberlain attend the forthcoming meeting. He fully realized, Drummond explained, the very great inconvenience of his request. He ventured, however, most earnestly to urge that Chamberlain endeavour to attend the forthcoming

---

A search of the Greek Foreign Ministry archives has failed to yield any report by Caclamanos on the interview with Sir Austen Chamberlain. Likewise, the British Foreign Office archives in the Public Record Office, London, has failed to show any such interview between Chamberlain and Caclamanos. Caclamanos's belief that Greece was dissuaded from further actions by this interview alone is open to question, as the following pages show.

[47] Caclamanos (London) to the F.Min., no. 2827, 23 Oct. 1925. Greek Archives.
[48] A meeting of the British Cabinet, 23 Oct. 1925. File CAB/23/51, PRO.

meeting personally because of the great importance of the question from the 'League of Nations point of view'. A serious challenge, he continued, had been made to the world organization, 'and all [the] other members of [the] League will watch with intense interest whether [the] League machinery can function adequately and speedily'. Chamberlain's presence would add enormously to the value of any Council decision and would have a profound effect on the Balkan situation generally. Drummond had scheduled the Council meeting at Paris for late Monday afternoon, which would give Chamberlain the possibility of leaving London that same morning.[49]

As a former member of the Foreign Office, Drummond was in a unique position to send such a communication and to take such an initiative. This move, however, as well as those that Drummond had taken when the incident had first come to the League's attention some days before, shows quite clearly that even the most non-political Secretary-General, as Drummond supposedly was, especially if one examines his powers under the pertinent sections of the League Covenant, can and does play an important political role in world affairs.

Drummond's communication had, of course, arrived after the Cabinet's decision to send Chamberlain to Paris had been made. In fact, Chamberlain received it that evening just before he was to depart for a week-end in the country. He thanked Drummond for his message and informed him that he would leave for the League Council's Paris meeting on the early train that coming Monday. The fact that he would attend the Council session might be publicized,[50] a move by Chamberlain no doubt intended to impress the military government in Athens, not to mention the anxious suppliants in Sofia.

[49] Drummond (Geneva) to the F.O., no. 379, 23 Oct. 1925. FO/800/258, PRO.
[50] Selby (London) to the British Consul at Geneva for Drummond, 23 Oct. 1925. FO/800/258, PRO.

IV

COERCION: SECOND PHASE

Moves in Athens and Sofia

WHILE these events were transpiring between London, Paris, and Rome, from the afternoon of 22 October until the following afternoon, other actions were taking place in Athens and Sofia.

On the morning of 23 October in Athens, the British Minister, Cheetham, called on his French colleague, Chambrun, and found that the latter had received instructions from Paris independent of those that Cheetham had received from London, but of such a nature as to allow Chambrun to act on the lines the Foreign Office had desired.[1] Acting as they had been instructed, they immediately called at the Italian Legation on the chargé d'affaires, Domenico de Facendis. They informed De Facendis of their governments' instructions: for each to contact his two other colleagues in order to take joint action towards the Greek Government, advising 'moderation' in the current dispute with the Bulgars.

They asked De Facendis, therefore, whether he had received instructions along these lines and whether he was inclined to act on similar lines. De Facendis replied that he had not yet received orders from Rome, but interpreting Mussolini's thoughts, which were always directed towards peace, he found no difficulty in associating himself with his British and French colleagues in advising 'calm and moderation' to the Greeks in their present dispute.[2]

Satisfied with De Facendis's reply, Cheetham hurried to the Greek Foreign Ministry, with the Italian chargé d'affaires following soon after. The British Minister called on Hadjikyriakos and 'urged him' to withdraw the advancing Greek forces to their own soil. By doing so an opportunity would be afforded for a truce, which in turn might be followed by an on-the-spot inquiry into the responsibilities for the incident. The Greek Foreign Minister responded 'quietly but firmly' that it was impossible for his country to surrender the strategic positions to which they were now advancing.

[1] Athens to the F.O., no. 165, 23 Oct. 1925. File 953, FO/286/916, PRO.
[2] Facendis (Athens) to Mussolini, 23 Oct. 1925. Italian Archives.

Instead, Hadjikyriakos insisted that Bulgarian forces were still in occupation of Greek territory. The interview had obviously got nowhere.

General Pangalos, Cheetham observed to London, was 'probably anxious for a success which will strengthen his political situation'. The French Minister, Chambrun, was to see General Pangalos that afternoon, and Cheetham would report as quickly as possible on the result of his interview with the Greek dictator. In the interim, he supposed that the situation would be changed by the Bulgarian decision to appeal to the League of Nations.[3]

While waiting for the Foreign Minister, Hadjikyriakos, De Facendis met Dantcheff, who explained that he had come to inform the Foreign Minister that, following the Greek advance into Bulgaria, his government had turned to the League of Nations.

De Facendis's interview began immediately after Cheetham's exit from Hadjikyriakos's office. As expected, the Foreign Minister repeated the Greek case made in Athens's note to Sofia, and explained that, to dislodge the Bulgarians from Greek territory, the military had decided to avoid a frontal attack which would have resulted in great loss of life, and instead chose to skirt the Bulgarian line, thus forcing the Bulgars to retire or be surrounded.

De Facendis observed that he had learned of the government's moderation in drawing up its note to Sofia and had been favourably impressed by this action. He had no doubts, he added, that the government would continue to be inspired by a desire for 'moderation of action' and for the 'serenity of judgment necessary' in order not to disturb the peace, which was ardently desired by all. Hadjikyriakos assured De Facendis that his government wished nothing from Bulgaria and asked only to be allowed to live in peace. It did not wish to be molested repeatedly by the troops of the regular Bulgarian Army, much less by komitadjis—actions for which the government in Sofia was responsible. He felt that Greece had suffered an unexpected aggression and invasion of its territory, and was obliged to defend itself. According to the Foreign Minister, Athens had a right to ask for a modest indemnity for the lives of the Greek soldiers unjustly murdered, and his government would not fail to defend itself before the League of Nations if it were asked by Geneva to state its reasons for invading Bulgaria.[4]

[3] Athens to the F.O., no. 165, 23 Oct. 1925. File 953, FO/286/916, PRO.
[4] Facendis (Athens) to Mussolini, 23 Oct. 1925. Italian Archives.

That afternoon, as arranged, the French Minister, Chambrun, had a long interview with the Prime Minister, General Pangalos. The greatest concession that he was able to get from Pangalos, Chambrun informed Cheetham, was a promise that the Greek forces would not advance any further into Bulgaria. It was Chambrun's belief that this comparative success was due only to the 'combined pressure exercised by [the] three Legations'.

Cheetham was convinced by his interview with Hadjikyriakos that the latter merely repeated Pangalos's orders. General Pangalos, the British Minister felt, would 'certainly make no further concessions' until the results of municipal elections, to take place the following day, were known. He agreed with Chambrun that 'diplomatic pressure will in any case produce no further effect'. The Greeks were, in fact, too suspicious of the Bulgars to give up any of the advantages of their position.[5]

In Sofia that day somewhat similar moves were taking place. The first news that Stevenson received was from the Bulgarian Foreign Ministry, stating that the Greek advance into Bulgaria was still continuing, but at a slower rate. In fact, contrary to the expectations of the Bulgars, Petrich had not yet been occupied. Furthermore, because of the Greek bombardment, the Bulgarian authorities were experiencing a considerable amount of difficulty in persuading the local population to remain in Petrich and in the villages adjacent to the scene of conflict.[6] When this information was received in the Foreign Office, Bateman minuted to Stevenson's communication that the 'weight of evidence [was] against Greece' on this issue.[7]

In the interim, Dantcheff in Athens informed the Bulgarian Foreign Ministry that the Greek Government was ignorant of the actual state of affairs at the frontier. In addition, inexplicably, General Pangalos had 'taken up [a] conciliatory attitude' maintaining that the protest note addressed to the Bulgars was in no sense an ultimatum. The Greek dictator suggested the dispatch to the frontier of an officer from the Greek General Staff to meet a Bulgarian officer arranging for a commission of inquiry. The Bulgars had decided, however, to reply to Pangalos that in so far as the matter had been referred to the League they could not negotiate

---

[5] Athens to the F.O., no. 166, 23 Oct. 1925. File 953, FO/286/916, PRO.
[6] Stevenson (Sofia) to the F.O., no. 81, 23 Oct. 1925. File 13309, FO/371/10672, PRO; Stevenson (Sofia) to Chamberlain, no. 231, 28 Oct. 1925. File 13309, FO/371/10673, PRO.
[7] Minute by C.H.B., 24 Oct. 1925. File 13309, FO/371/10672, PRO.

directly with the Greeks so long as a single Greek soldier was to be found on Bulgarian territory.

Sofia had also been informed from Athens by a reliable source that orders for the advance into Bulgaria had not been given by the Greek General Staff, but that it had been left to the commander at Salonika to take the steps he thought necessary to deal with the frontier incident. If this information was true, Stevenson observed, it 'would appear to be [a] convenient loophole for possible future use' by the Athens government.[8]

During the course of that morning, 23 October, Stevenson received what was to be the first of several disturbing reports. From a reliable source—a euphemism for a controlled British intelligence informant—he ascertained that the Bulgarian General Staff was concentrating troops in the area of the Struma Valley defile. He also learned from the Yugoslav Legation that members of the Macedonian Revolutionary Organization—the Bulgarian komitadji organization—were proceeding under orders to the scene of the conflict. The Yugoslav Legation in Sofia, however, could not be regarded as the most impartial source as far as komitadji activities were concerned. Moreover, the report received was circumstantial, and the action of the komitadjis appeared to be only what would naturally be taken by them.[9]

At this point Stevenson received the Foreign Office's instructions sent the previous day. In view of the situation that now appeared to be developing as a result of the komitadji movements, he decided to intervene with the Bulgarian Government. While renewing his counsel of moderation given previously, Stevenson would let the Bulgars know that London was advocating intervention in a similar sense in Athens. His first move, however, before proceeding to the Bulgarian Foreign Ministry, was to consult with his French and Italian colleagues. Both the French Minister, Dard, and the Italian chargé, Leone, agreed with Stevenson that the knowledge that the British Government advocated intervention in Athens might strengthen the resolve of the Bulgarian Government to persevere in its attitude of non-resistance to the Greek invasion,

---

[8] Sofia to Athens, addressed to the F.O., no. 82, repeated to Belgrade, 23 Oct. 1925. File 953, FO/286/916, PRO; Stevenson (Sofia) to Chamberlain, no. 231, 28 Oct. 1925. File 13309, FO/371/10673, PRO.

[9] Stevenson (Sofia) to Chamberlain, no. 231, 28 Oct. 1925. File 13309, FO/371/10673, PRO.

which the Bulgars had insisted they had maintained until then. Stevenson therefore went to the Foreign Ministry to call on Kalfoff. While waiting for Kalfoff, he was soon joined by Dard, who informed Stevenson that he had received instructions from Paris showing that his government had taken an initiative similar to that of the British Government in proposing joint intervention at Athens and Sofia. Accordingly Stevenson, now joined by Dard, called on the Bulgarian Foreign Minister and together they made joint representations. They explained to Kalfoff that both their governments had the intention of intervening in Athens and that the statements of their governments evidently recognized the correctness of the Bulgarian Government's attitude in expressing its willingness to agree to a joint Greek-Bulgarian commission of inquiry over the incident. Stevenson and Dard expressed their 'fervent hopes' that the Bulgars would continue to avoid at all costs any hostile action against the Greeks.

Replying, Kalfoff expressed the gratitude of his government towards the British and French Governments for their prompt response to Sofia's appeal made to them by the Bulgarian Ministers in London and Paris. He drew Stevenson's and Dard's attention to the fact that the Greek military had renewed their advance at midday. On Stevenson's and Dard's request, however, Kalfoff gave a solemn pledge on behalf of his government that orders previously given to the Bulgarian military to retire in the face of the Greek advance, and as far as possible avoid contact with them, would be strictly maintained.

Kalfoff warned them, however, that in the event of the Greeks pursuing their advance into the heart of Bulgaria or committing acts of particular cruelty or bombing interior towns from the air, the Bulgarian Government would have to reconsider its attitude. Questioned as to the attitude Sofia would assume should Petrich be occupied, Kalfoff assured Stevenson and Dard that such an event would in no way alter the determination of his government to avoid hostilities with the Greeks.

During the course of this conversation Kalfoff impressed upon his British and French interviewers that the Bulgarian Government regarded the whole affair as falling under his competence alone, and that therefore the Ministry of War was acting under his instructions. Asked by the British chargé about the concentration of Bulgarian troops at the defile of the Struma Valley, Kalfoff denied any such concentration, 'but gave the impression' to both Stevenson and Dard that 'he was lying'.

In the middle of this interview, word arrived that the League Council would convene on Monday, 26 October, in Paris. Kalfoff was deeply gratified by the speed of the response to his appeal. He begged Stevenson and Dard to transmit to their governments Sofia's earnest entreaties that London, Paris, and Rome should in the interim intervene in the Greek capital with the purpose of stopping the Greek advance and if possible to persuade them to withdraw from Bulgarian territory.

Stevenson had gathered, from both his conversation with Kalfoff and one with Minkoff, that the Bulgarian Foreign Ministry was having 'not a little difficulty' in restraining the martial ardour of the Bulgarian Ministry of War.[10]

It was Stevenson's opinion that the 'danger [was] real' that even if the Bulgarian military obeyed orders not to resist the Greek advance, the komitadjis would 'attack [the] invading force and provoke reprisals which might precipitate [a] general conflict'. He mentioned Kalfoff's and Minkoff's difficulties with the Bulgarian military and Kalfoff's less than candid answer when questioned about the troop concentrations in the defile of the Struma Valley. The Greek chargé, Rosetti, Stevenson also informed the Foreign Office, was completely in the dark at the disobedience of the Greek military to their orders to halt the advance into Bulgaria and was communicating with Athens and Salonika for explanations. Stevenson considered it 'absolutely essential that pressure be brought to bear on [the] Greek Government to stay their advance immediately'.[11] The arrival of this communication at the Foreign Office prompted Bateman to minute: 'All the more reason for renewed representations at Athens'.[12] This report from Stevenson was soon followed by one from the British Minister in Belgrade, Kennard, who informed the Foreign Office that the Yugoslav Foreign Minister, Ninčić, had expressed the conviction that any Greek advance on Petrich, 'a hotbed of Macedonian intrigue, must result

[10] Sofia to Athens, addressed to the F.O., no. 84, repeated to Belgrade, Bucharest, Rome, and Constantinople, 23 Oct. 1925. File 953, FO/286/916, PRO; Stevenson (Sofia) to Chamberlain, no. 231, 28 Oct. 1925. File 13309, FO/371/10673, PRO.
[11] Stevenson (Sofia) to the F.O., no. 86, 23 Oct. 1925. File 13309, FO/371/10672, PRO.
[12] Minute by C.H.B., 24 Oct. 1925. File 13309, FO/371/10672, PRO.

in war', and if war did erupt he was of the opinion that the Bulgars would within a short period take Salonika and Alexandroupolis.[13] This news from Belgrade caused Bateman to minute again that it suited the Yugoslavs to maintain that the Bulgars would defeat the Greeks in a general action—although there was little doubt that the Bulgars would do so if they were to have access to sufficient artillery. 'The danger from the Macedonians [was] however very real. The Greeks [were] asking for trouble', he concluded.[14] The danger of komitadji involvement and the further complication of what was by now a very complicated situation was beginning to worry the Central Department of the Foreign Office.

Late in the afternoon the news conveyed to Stevenson by Rosetti was that the Greek advance had again stopped. This information was soon contradicted by the Bulgarian Foreign Ministry and the correspondent of *The Times* of London, who telephoned Stevenson from Petrich, then under fairly heavy shelling. He informed Stevenson that a large Greek force was reported to be advancing on the town. The inhabitants of Petrich were in a state of great indignation and very excited. Resistance to the Greek advance was being made by a body of regular Bulgarian soldiers and militia—the latter komitadjis 'thinly disguised'. This was the only first-hand evidence that Stevenson had of Bulgarian resistance.

By the evening of 23 October, Briand's communication in his capacity as Acting President of the League Council, calling on Athens and Sofia to suspend hostilities and withdraw their forces, reached the Bulgarian authorities. According to the Bulgars orders were immediately given to the Bulgarian military to cease even the small amount of rifle fire in which they had indulged up to that point.[15]

That day the Bulgarians had not been diplomatically inactive. Desirous of the widest support, and doubtless still unsure whether their appeal to the League would invoke a positive response, indirect contact was established with the German Legation in Sofia. As the German Minister, Eugen Rümelin, explained to Berlin, Raschko Madjaroff, the Minister of Justice and an influential member of the Bulgarian Cabinet, had addressed him by way of

---

[13] Kennard (Belgrade) to the F.O., no. 137, 23 Oct. 1925. File 13309, FO/371/10672, PRO.

[14] Minute by C.H.B., 24 Oct. 1925. File 13309, FO/371/10672, PRO.

[15] Stevenson (Sofia) to Chamberlain, no. 231, 28 Oct. 1925. File 13309, FO/371/10673, PRO.

a third party and asked his personal advice as to what the govern-ment should do. Rümelin tendered the same advice as his British, French, and Italian colleagues: withdraw the Bulgarian troops in order not to spoil the present favourable impression made by Bulgaria abroad. Because of her demilitarization, military superio-rity was clearly on the Greek side, and therefore Sofia should concentrate on an 'energetic political and press campaign abroad'. Madjaroff, Rümelin added, was especially interested in ascertaining Chancellor Gustav Stresemann's personal interpretation of the whole situation.[16] Stresemann agreed completely with Rümelin's advice to Madjaroff and felt that, despite Germany's friendship with Bulgaria, it was inadvisable to tender advice at this moment in view of the impending intervention of the League of Nations, to which Sofia had by now appealed.[17] Thus, the Germans had adopted the same attitude as the British, French, and Italians, and Bulgarian approaches to the Wilhelmstrasse had been rejected.

Nor had Rome been forgotten. That day Minkoff had had an interview with Leone, who had not joined Stevenson and Dard in their talk with Kalfoff, since he had not received his instructions—which, as we have seen, did not arrive from Mussolini until the following day, 24 October. Minkoff explained to the Italian chargé that the Anglo-French representatives had invited the Bulgarian Government 'to abstain in [a] positive manner from any resistance or act that will complicate the already grave situation further'. Minkoff, however, ominously warned Leone that, though the Cabinet had confirmed the orders to the military to retire without offering resistance, the Great Powers must be convinced that the Bulgarian troops would not continue to endure the Greek advance passively. In fact, the Macedonian population of the invaded region might at any moment revolt against the Greeks, provoking a conflict of greater proportions. The Cabinet, he revealed, had also refused to discuss with the Athens government its ultimatum as

<hr/>

[16] Rümelin (Sofia) to the Reichsminister personally, 23 Oct. 1925. Microfilms of the German Foreign Ministry Archives 1920–45, Serial Number L39, Roll 4021, Frame Numbers Lo11149–Lo11150, NA.

[17] Stresemann (Berlin) to Rümelin (Sofia), 25 Oct. 1925. Microfilms of the German Foreign Ministry Archives 1920–45, Serial Number L39, Roll 4021, Frame Numbers Lo11151–Lo11152, NA. The substance of Stresemann's answer was also repeated to the German Minister in Athens on 28 Oct. 1925. Microfilms of the German Foreign Ministry Archives 1920–45, Serial Number L39, Roll 4021, Frame Numbers Lo11153–Lo11154, NA.

long as Greek troops remained on Bulgarian territory. According to Minkoff, Sofia was relying on the League and the Great Powers to provide a solution to the conflict. The latter could help by intervening at Athens immediately in order to make the Greeks halt their advance[18]—a not oversubtle hint to the Italian Government.

The decision of the Bulgarian Government to maintain its passive role was immediately relayed to Athens by the Greek chargé, Rosetti.[19] Ever watchful of developing events in Sofia, he also divulged that his British colleague, Stevenson, had learned from the Foreign Office that the 'English Government [had] telegraphed [to] Rome [and] Paris [in order] that [the] three Powers intervene [collectively at] Sofia [and] Athens'. Accordingly the Allied representatives had that afternoon, the twenty-third, called on the Foreign Minister, Kalfoff, and passed on their governments' views. The Foreign Minister informed them that Bulgaria's attitude would change only if the Greek Army attempted to attack with greater force.[20] Rosetti also informed Athens, that the Yugoslav chargé d'affaires in Sofia, who had spoken with Kalfoff, had the impression that the Bulgarians would maintain their passive position 'if we stop our advance'. The Yugoslav's personal view was that, since Greece had already given the Bulgars a lesson, any further military action would only 'impair Greece's diplomatic position'. He also revealed to Rosetti that, in conversation with the representatives of the Great Powers, they had 'adversely' criticized the Greek attitude.[21]

Later that day, after all these messages had been dispatched to Athens, Rosetti received from the Bulgarian Foreign Ministry a reply to the Greek note received the previous day. As was to be expected, the Bulgars denied in the 'most categorical manner' the origins of the border incident as developed in Athens' note. Taking into consideration, however, that between both governments there was dispute as to fact, the Bulgarian Government had proposed from the very first that a commision *ad hoc* be instituted to proceed with an impartial inquiry. This proposition had been proffered twice to the Greek chargé d'affaires at Sofia and once to the government in Athens by the Bulgarian chargé d'affaires. Simultaneously,

[18] Weill Schott [Leone] (Sofia) to Mussolini, 23 Oct. 1925. Italian Archives.
[19] Rosetti (Sofia) to the F.Min., 23 Oct. 1925. Greek Archives.
[20] Rosetti (Sofia) to the F.Min., no. 1784, 23 Oct. 1925. Greek Archives.
[21] Rosetti (Sofia) to the F.Min., no. 1786, 23 Oct. 1925. Greek Archives.

the government in Sofia had requested that 'categorical orders' be given to both sides in order to stop the firing along the frontier. Unfortunately, this proposition had never been answered. Instead, Greek troops in considerable numbers had crossed the Bulgarian frontier attacking on a thirty-two-kilometre front and penetrating to a depth of about twelve kilometres. This invasion of the territory of a friendly nation, a League member, and a country well known to be disarmed, 'was accompanied by veritable acts of war'; including the use of infantry, artillery, and aircraft.

Because of the situation that had developed, the Bulgarian Government thought it necessary to appeal to the League of Nations, invoking Articles 10 and 11 of the Covenant, and asking for an immediate convening of the Council to deal with the situation. While waiting for the Council's decision and because the Greek Army continued to occupy Bulgarian soil, the government in Sofia, to its great regret, found it impossible to 'enter into direct negotiations with the Greek Government'.[22] On these grounds, to wit, the impossibility of direct talks between Greece and Bulgaria because the League was considering the issue, Sofia refused to reply to subsequent notes from Athens tendered by Rosetti on 23, 24, and 25 October.[23]

Further Instructions

Referring to Stevenson's messages about what had transpired in Sofia, Cheetham on the following day, 24 October, informed the Foreign Office that Athens had now agreed to evacuate the Bulgarian territory they had occupied. They would do this as soon as Greek troops were in a position to occupy their own frontier posts. If they were unable to do so as a result of Bulgarian action, they would appeal to the League.[24] This Greek assurance, he explained, had been given that morning to the French Minister, Chambrun, but Cheetham did not feel certain that it was of 'any great value'. General Pangalos, he observed, was at any rate paying more atten-

[22] *Note verbale* no. 2849, from the Bulgarian Foreign Ministry to the Greek Legation at Sofia, 23 Oct. 1925. Political 1925, League of Nations Archives; Rosetti (Sofia) to the F.Min., no. 1796, 24 Oct. 1925. French Text. Greek Archives.

[23] Ministère des Affaires Étrangères (Bulgarie), Récapitulation des événements concernant l'incident gréco-bulgare de Demir-Kapia jusqu'au moment de l'intervention du Conseil de la Société des Nations. Political 1925, League of Nations Archives.

[24] Athens to the F.O., no. 167, 24 Oct. 1925. File 953, FO/286/916, PRO.

tion to his and Chambrun's remonstrances.[25] Cheetham also agreed with Stevenson's communication that a komitadji attack, even if the Bulgarian military obeyed orders not to resist the Greek advance, was likely to hamper the efforts of the Bulgars and the Greeks to withdraw their forces, and constituted a real danger which the Athens government was not in a position to cope with. Indeed, the Yugoslav Minister in Athens had given Cheetham a warning of this kind, the result of the minister's experience with komitadji activity on the Yugoslav-Bulgar frontier in past years.[26]

These reports from Athens were matched by more satisfactory news from Sofia, which was improving its position: this was the expected Bulgarian acceptance of Briand's appeal. In his reply, Kalfoff expressed 'deep gratitude' on behalf of his government for the speed with which the League Council and Secretariat had acted. His own government, conscious of its obligations as a League member, had from the inception of the incident 'given the strictest orders' to the Bulgarian military to 'take no action which might make the situation worse'. 'Fresh instructions' to this effect had been immediately repeated, in accordance with Briand's communication, though Greek territory had not been violated by the Bulgarian Army. In conclusion, Kalfoff pointed out that Greek troops were still on Bulgarian soil and their artillery was bombarding the open sity of Petrich. Protesting against this behaviour, he begged Briand to 'intervene as soon as possible'.[27]

Further unsatisfactory information from Athens soon followed. The Greek reply of the same day, in spite of the representations of the Great Powers, was not, as the Foreign Office would have wanted, a complete acceptance of Briand's appeal. Hadjikyriakos felt that Sofia's version was at variance with the actual facts, and that 'the sudden and unprovoked character of the Bulgarian aggression' was obvious. His government therefore had to 'allow its military command to take all measures considered necessary for the defence and, if necessary, the clearance of its national territory', at that very moment still occupied by Bulgarian forces. Orders at the same time had been issued that bloodshed should be avoided and the population safeguarded if the defensive measures of the Greek

[25] Sir M.C. (Athens) to the F.O., no. 168, 24 Oct. 1925. File 953, FO/286/916, PRO.
[26] Sir M.C. (Athens) to the F.O., no. 169, 24 Oct. 1925. File 953, FO/286/916, PRO.
[27] Text. League of Nations, *Official Journal*, 6th year, 1925, p. 1697.

Army led to military operations on Bulgarian territory. However, Hadjikyriakos noted, at that very moment Bulgarian fire continued 'with the purpose of preventing us from re-occupying our two frontier posts'. When these posts had been re-occupied and the whole area freed, Greek troops would withdraw to the Greek frontier line, 'provided that no fresh intervention of regular troops or [komitadji] bands takes place'. The Greek Government therefore felt that the measures undertaken by its military were nothing more than 'measures of legitimate defence and could not be considered as hostile acts likely to lead to a rupture in accordance with the terms of Article 12 of the Covenant'.

Because of this, Article 12 could not be invoked in the present question. Nevertheless, Hadjikyriakos ended, Athens, 'strong and confident in the justice of its cause and in deference to the League of Nations, will . . . accept the competence of the Council in this matter'.[28]

Later that day, in Paris, Jules Laroche in a discussion with the Greek Minister, Carapanos, recommended that Athens accept a solution by the League Council. He pointed out that the Bulgarian declaration not to oppose the advance of the Greek forces as long as they did not exceed their present line of occupation had produced among 'official circles [a] good impression'. In reply, Carapanos limited himself to a mere reiteration of his government's reports refuting the Bulgarian charges. The minister's own impression was that the interview had been dictated by Geneva, feeling 'uneasiness' over Hadjikyriakos's ambiguous reply.[29]

From London, the Greek Minister was also reporting important and interesting information. According to the general opinion prevailing in the British capital, Caclamanos informed Athens, the League Council would insist on both nations withdrawing their forces across their respective frontiers. Simultaneously, a neutral zone would be fixed and a neutral military committee appointed to investigate the incident. The question of damages, he explained, would be examined only after the report of the committee had been issued.[30] His second telegram, however, contained an ominous warning: a member of the Cabinet, Lord Robert Cecil, had given a

---

[28] Ibid.
[29] Carapanos (Paris) to the F.Min., no. 4880, 24 Oct. 1925. Greek Archives.
[30] Caclamanos (London) to the F.Min., no. 2830, 24 Oct. 1925. Greek Archives.

speech in Scotland touching on the dispute. According to Cecil, both Bulgaria and Greece were honourable countries and League members. He was convinced that in the desire to fulfil their obligations—accepting discussion or arbitration before the League of Nations—they would never resort to war. However, if war did come, the League was duty bound to 'take measures against the attacker'. The first measure would be the breaking of diplomatic relations with the attacking state by all fifty-two members of the League. If the attacking state still did not yield, the next step would be to halt all commercial relations. Lord Robert hoped and believed that neither Athens nor Sofia would 'break the Covenant [of the] League of Nations', but if they did, the League would quickly apply Article 16 of the Covenant[31]—dealing with the imposition of economic sanctions against an aggressor state. Since the speech had been made by one of Greece's staunchest supporters during the Corfu Incident of two years earlier,[32] British determination to use the League machinery if matters deteriorated further must have impressed Athens and the Greek Foreign Ministry.

Advice that the Greeks submit completely to the League Council was also reported by Rosetti, in Sofia. The French Minister, Dard, in conversation with him, had maintained that it was unquestionably in the interests of Greece to 'conform' with Briand's appeal, 'thus establishing her diplomatic position'. These thoughts were also echoed by the British chargé, Stevenson.[33] Rosetti further reported that his Yugoslav colleague had expressed the view that, once the League had agreed to consider the question, the continuation of military measures by Greece against Bulgaria was harmful to her interests and strengthened world public opinion against her. Moreover, in Sofia's diplomatic circles, Greek actions were being criticized 'adversely', especially after Hadjikyriakos's evasive telegram

[31] Caclamanos (London) to the F.Min., no. 2839, 24 Oct. 1925. Greek Archives.

[32] In late August of 1923, the Italian members of an international commission de-limiting the Greek-Albanian frontier were murdered by person or persons unknown. Mussolini's immediate reaction had been to dispatch an ultimatum to Greece and to bombard and occupy the Greek island of Corfu. Athens's appeal to the League and the Greek position in general was strongly supported by Lord Robert Cecil, who at that time was Britain's representative to the League Council. The question, however, was finally settled not by the League but by the Conference of Ambassadors sitting in Paris. See James Barros, *The Corfu Incident of 1923: Mussolini and the League of Nations* (Princeton University Press, 1965).

[33] Rosetti (Sofia) to the F.Min., no. 1795, 24 Oct. 1925. Greek Archives.

to Briand. As to the internal Bulgarian situation, Rosetti anxiously noted that, according to information reaching him, King Boris had appealed to the Macedonians to listen to the orders of the government as Bulgaria endured this 'critical hour'.[34]

While Rosetti was reporting to Athens, across the city his Italian colleague, Leone, was communicating with Rome. He revealed to Mussolini that both Stevenson and Dard were keeping him abreast of the instructions and reports that they received from their respective governments, and that on his part he was maintaining continuous contact with them.[35] The arrival of Mussolini's instructions earlier that day, to act in concert with the French and British representatives,[36] had caused the Italian chargé to seek an immediate interview with Minkoff at the Foreign Ministry. On arrival Leone repeated his previous 'counsel for moderation'. He explained that Rome, in company with Paris and London, while requesting the Bulgarian Government to maintain an attitude of calm, had also turned to Athens in order to resolve the incident in a just manner. In reply, Minkoff stated that his government had reached their limit in showing calm. He revealed to Leone that an hour before he had received notice from the Bulgarian General Staff that the Greeks had resumed the bombardment of Petrich and other villages that morning. He pointed out that Sofia, responding to the message sent by Briand, 'had once again manifested its deep desire for peace and its trust in [the] work of the League of Nations'. Ending his report to Rome, Leone noted that Minkoff had emphasized the fact that the resumed artillery fire was concentrated on defenceless villages and territory.[37]

In Athens, De Facendis, like Leone, also received his instructions dispatched earlier that day and informed his French and British colleagues accordingly. He felt that the advice for moderation collectively recommended by the Great Powers to the Greeks had not been without effect and that the incident could be said to have passed the 'critical and disquieting stage'. He reported that acts of hostility had ceased and that, with Hadjikyriakos's communication to Briand, the question had been 'deferred to the examination and judgment of the League of Nations'.[38] De Facendis's

[34] Rosetti (Sofia) to the F.Min., no. 1802, 24 Oct. 1925. Greek Archives.
[35] Weill Schott [Leone] (Sofia) to Mussolini, 24 Oct. 1925. Italian Archives.
[36] *Supra*, Chapter III.
[37] Weill Schott [Leone] (Sofia) to Mussolini, 24 Oct. 1925. Italian Archives.
[38] Facendis (Athens) to Mussolini, 24 Oct. 1925. Italian Archives.

optimistic predictions, however, were premature, as events on the Greek-Bulgarian frontier, as well as between London, Athens, and Sofia, revealed.

In London that morning, 24 October, the Bulgarian Minister, Misheff, appeared at the Foreign Office and called on Lampson at the Central Department. Lampson at that point had not yet received Stevenson's report dispatched the previous day, in which he warned that komitadji involvement and a widening of the struggle was a real danger. Lampson was therefore disinclined to accept Misheff's suggestion that the Foreign Office should again send instructions to Cheetham in Athens. The arrival of Stevenson's warning, however, coupled with Misheff's request seemed to Lampson 'to justify immediate action'. Since time was short and the matter was urgent, he sent further instructions to Cheetham in Athens, which he trusted would receive Chamberlain's subsequent approval.[39] He entirely approved Lampson's action, Chamberlain minuted. The Foreign Secretary scribbled that he had 'felt the greatest sympathy with Greece and watched for an opportunity to help her effectively'. But Pangalos's government was putting Greece 'outside the pale'. Chamberlain observed that he would try his 'utmost in the interest of everyone (not excluding Greece) to get a clear and decisive verdict from the Council of the League'.[40]

Lampson's instructions to Cheetham explained that Misheff had called at the Foreign Office that morning with instructions from Sofia dated the previous night, 23 October. In effect, the Bulgarians alleged that Greek forces were still moving forward, east of the Struma river. Under these circumstances, the Bulgarian Government was afraid of incidents developing for which they would disclaim all responsibility. Sofia therefore begged that the British Government urge Athens to suspend all forward movement of its troops. The Foreign Office, however, in reply, had cautioned Misheff that previous orders to the Bulgarian military not to resist should not be rescinded. These instructions, assuming they were reported correctly, had strengthened the Bulgarian case. The Bulgarian Minister was reminded that in Sofia's original appeal to Geneva invoking the League's assistance, it had been emphatically stated that the orders not to resist the invading Greeks had been

---

[39] Minute by M. W. Lampson, 24 Oct. 1925. File 13309, FO/371/10672, PRO.

[40] Minute by Sir A.C., 24 Oct. 1925. File 13309, FO/371/10672, PRO.

re-affirmed. Thus, any modification of these orders 'would be most unfortunate'. In reply, Misheff denied that any such action was intended.

It was also pointed out to Misheff that the whole question was now in the hands of the League Council and therefore it was difficult for 'an individual government to take further action such as [that] suggested by [the] Bulgarian Government'. Furthermore, Briand, as Acting President of the League Council, had already reminded both nations, in his communication of the previous day, of their obligation as League members, under Article 12 of the Covenant, not to go to war. He had also warned Bulgaria and Greece of the grave consequences, under the terms of the League's Covenant, which would develop from any violation of Article 12 of the Covenant.

But apart from that, the British, French, and Italian diplomatic representatives both at Athens and Sofia had received general instructions to exercise such restraining influence upon both states as was possible. Because of this it appeared to the Foreign Office unnecessary to convey further specific instructions to Athens as desired by Sofia.

However, it was explained to Cheetham, since the above conversation had taken place with Misheff, Stevenson's warning had been received about possible komitadji involvement and a resultant widening of the conflict. This possible development doubtlessly explained the instructions upon which Misheff was acting. Cheetham was therefore ordered to see his French and Italian colleagues immediately, informing them of the information the Foreign Office had received and of Misheff's request. He was to endeavour to get Chambrun's and De Facendis's support and to warn the Athens government immediately of the 'folly' of any forward advance by their troops, pending a decision by the League Council. The Greeks should realize that contravention of Article 12 of the League Covenant 'might well have the most serious consequences for them'.[41]

---

[41] F.O. to Cheetham, no. 129, 24 Oct. 1925. File 13309, FO/371/10672, PRO.
   At about the same time that Misheff was appearing at the Foreign Office, the French Minister in Sofia, Dard, was conversing with the correspondent of *Le Matin*. According to Dard, the conduct of the Bulgarian Government had produced an 'excellent impression' at the Quai d'Orsay. This was especially true since Sofia by 'neglecting certain counsels' had immediately taken the path of Geneva and Locarno and appealed to the Council of the League of Nations. (Felix de Gérando, *L'Incident Gréco-Bulgare d'Octobre 1925* (Sofia, 1926), pp. 26-7.)

Stevenson's fears had, of course, been well justified by the continuing military preparations of the Bulgarian Army, as well as the movements of komitadji bands towards the area of conflict, all mirrored in the apprehensions of King Boris, Kalfoff, and Minkoff.[42] As to the renewed hostilities on the frontier, an answer was supplied by the American chargé d'affaires, Cable. It appears that at eight o'clock that morning 'all [such] firing as the Bulgarians had been engaging in, totally ceased'. Later in the afternoon 'the Greeks were observed to be packing up', and the Bulgarian Foreign Ministry was reporting that the incident was over. However, at 5.30 in the late afternoon, Greek artillery fire was resumed. The Yugoslav military attaché in Sofia, Colonel Milkovitch, after examining the situation, considered that the Bulgarians were preventing the Greeks from occupying their frontier posts until a neutral commission could examine the spot, to ascertain on which side of the frontier line the corpse of the dead Greek sentry was to be found.[43]

It was in the midst of these developments that Cheetham received his new orders from the Foreign Office. As instructed, he endeavoured to contact his French and Italian colleagues. But Cheetham found that 'both of them considered their role terminated', since the whole question was now in the hands of the League of Nations. Indeed, the French Minister, Chambrun, had left the Greek capital for the day. However, in view of his instructions Cheetham called on Hadjikyriakos, the Foreign Minister, and spent an hour talking to him as well as to the Prime Minister, General Pangalos. He asked General Pangalos what news he had from the Greek-Bulgarian frontier. Pangalos repeated that the Greek Government was ready to evacuate the Bulgarian territory they had occupied as soon as Greek troops were in a position to occupy their own frontier posts. He maintained that the Greek military could not retreat safely in view of the positions that the Bulgars occupied. Cheetham then asked him specifically whether, that being the case, he had appealed to the League Council and had stated the reasons which prevented the Greek Army from withdrawing from Bulgaria. Pangalos replied that he had done so.

[42] During this period there were a number of reports from Rosetti, the Greek chargé d'affaires in Sofia, reporting to Athens the military preparations of the Bulgarian Army, and the activities and movements of komitadji organizations. Greek Archives.

[43] Cable (Sofia) to the Dept. of State, 26 Oct. 1925. File 768.74/232, Record Group 59, NA.

Cheetham then gave the Greek Prime Minister 'a serious but friendly warning' on the lines of the last sentence of the Foreign Office's instructions. Pangalos insisted that Bulgarian troops were occupying Greek territory and that under these circumstances the Greek Army was unable to retire safely to the Greek frontier. He maintained that he would be able to explain the situation that had developed to the satisfaction of the League Council.[44] Cheetham observed to the Foreign Office that Pangalos appeared to have spoken 'sincerely' to him, but Cheetham 'did not feel quite sure' that the General had 'put the whole situation' before him.[45]

This interview between Cheetham and the Greek leaders ended the day's events. On the following day, 25 October, Stevenson in Sofia reported to the Foreign Office that the Greek bombardment still continued intermittently. From a village near Petrich the correspondent of *The Times* of London reported to Stevenson by telephone that not only the local population but also the Bulgarian military 'were getting into a state of dangerous excitement'. The question was how long the Bulgars would continue to submit to the Greek bombardment without retaliating. The situation was hourly becoming more dangerous. Although the Bulgarian Government affirmed its attitude of non-resistance to the Greek advance, they emphasized that this position was becoming increasingly difficult as each minute passed in view of the continued Greek shelling.[46] Furthermore Kalfoff admitted to Stevenson for the first time that military reinforcements, including artillery, had been moved towards the frontier, while Minkoff hinted that there were now sufficient Bulgarian troops concentrated in the south to deal with the Greeks.[47] When this news reached London, Bateman

[44] Athens to the F.O., no. 171, 24 Oct. 1925. File 953, FO/286/916, PRO.

[45] Sir M.C. (Athens) to the F.O., no. 172, 24 Oct. 1925. File 953, FO/286/916, PRO.

[46] Stevenson (Sofia) to the F.O., no. 89, 25 Oct. 1925. File 13309, FO/371/10672, PRO; Stevenson (Sofia) to Chamberlain, no. 231, 28 Oct. 1925. File 13309, FO/371/10673, PRO.

[47] Stevenson (Sofia) to Chamberlain, no. 231, 28 Oct. 1925. File 13309, FO/371/10673, PRO.

On that day, 25 October, the British Legation in Athens was informed that Philippe Berthelot, the Secretary-General of the French Foreign Ministry, appeared confident that the situation was in hand. Berthelot had 'stated at mid-day today that Bulgaria had withdrawn from Greek territory and that [the] Greeks had agreed to withdraw from Bulgarian territory'. Moreover, he had no anxieties as to the pacific intentions of the Yugoslav Government. (Paris to Athens, 25 Oct. 1925. File 953, FO/286/916, PRO.)

supposed that, now that the League had the question in hand, the Foreign Office could do nothing. The Greeks, however, needed 'the heavy stick well applied and the sooner the better'.[48] Bateman's colleague in the Central Department, Howard Smith, agreed, and understood that Chamberlain was 'quite ready to apply it'.[49]

According to Stevenson, 'the situation gave reason for considerable anxiety', and he determined to carry out an idea which had occurred to him on reading Hadjikyriakos's reply to Briand's telegram. It appeared to Stevenson that the crux of the situation lay in the area around the Greek frontier posts. According to Hadjikyriakos's note, the Greeks were prepared to withdraw their forces as soon as they were in a position to reoccupy their frontier posts to which access was denied them by Bulgarian fire from adjacent posts across the frontier line. Since the Greek and Bulgarian posts on this section of the line were situated on top of a ridge only thirty yards apart, Stevenson realized that the Greeks would not dare approach their own posts for fear of coming under Bulgarian fire, even supposing that the passivity of the Bulgarian troops on the spot was all that the government in Sofia claimed that it was. However, if the Bulgarians could be persuaded to withdraw their troops from the area, the Athens government would have no further excuse for occupying Bulgarian territory.

Stevenson therefore decided to consult with his French and Italian colleagues with a view to persuading the Bulgars to withdraw their troops from these frontier posts, which appeared to have no strategic value. By agreeing, the Bulgars would deprive the Athens government of its last excuse for continuing its occupation of Bulgarian territory. The French Minister, Dard, agreed immediately to join Stevenson in giving a 'personal suggestion' along these lines to the Bulgarian Government. However, the Italian chargé, Leone, 'was extremely unwilling', as he had been throughout the affair, Stevenson observed, to take any initiative without specific instructions from Rome.

It transpired in the course of their discussions that the Bulgars' great anxiety to retain possession of their frontier posts was due to the fact that behind one of these posts lay the body of the Greek soldier whose death had ignited the incident. Eventually it was

[48] Minute by C.H.B., 26 Oct. 1925. File 13309, FO/371/10672, PRO.
[49] Minute by C. Howard Smith, 26 Oct. 1925. File 13309, FO/371/10672, PRO.

agreed that they should call on Kalfoff and endeavour to obtain from him an admission as to the facts, and, if possible, they were to suggest the withdrawal of the Bulgarian troops from the frontier posts. When they called on Kalfoff, they made it clear that they were acting without instructions. The Bulgarian Foreign Minister, however, readily admitted that the presence of the Greek soldier's body was the deciding factor in the Bulgarian troops' retention of the frontier posts in question. When it was pointed out to him that he had never previously mentioned this fact—not even when he asked that the Inter-Allied Military Organ of Liquidation should be authorized to proceed to the scene of the conflict—Kalfoff acknowledged this, but gave no explanation for this action. When asked whether the Bulgarian troops would withdraw once the presence of the Greek body on the Bulgarian side of the frontier had been definitely established by a neutral observer, Kalfoff replied that in that event, not only would Bulgarian forces be withdrawn from the frontier posts, but no opposition would be offered to their occupation by the Greek military, should the latter think such a move necessary to the safety of their army.

Once the interview with Kalfoff was over, Dard immediately dispatched a telegram to Briand, requesting that it should also be communicated to Chamberlain and to Italy's League Council representative, Vittorio Scialoja. In his communication to Briand, Dard suggested the appointment of Colonel Scanagatta as the neutral observer desired by Kalfoff. To this communication, Stevenson and Leone concurred. Dard and Stevenson, however, were of the opinion that, to be really effective, the action they had proposed should be taken immediately. Had this been done, the Bulgars might have withdrawn from the frontier posts by ten o'clock the following morning, as the neutral observer, leaving Sofia that night, Sunday, 25 October, could have reached the frontier by dawn of Monday. Leone, however, would not consent to anything more than the reference of their proposal to the League Council, and, in order not to draw Kalfoff's attention to their lack of agreement on this issue, Dard and Stevenson were forced to acquiesce, thus losing valuable time, 'every minute of which was fraught with dangerous possibilities'.[50]

[50] Stevenson (Sofia) to the F.O., no. 90, 25 Oct. 1925. File 13309, FO/371/10672, PRO; Stevenson (Sofia) to Chamberlain, no. 231, 28 Oct. 1925. File 13309, FO/371/10673, PRO.

Bateman at the Foreign Office minuted to this report that to certify that the Greek corpse was behind a Bulgar blockhouse *now* proved nothing—unless they were to presume that the fire between the Greek and Bulgar frontier posts at thirty yards' range was so hot that no one had dared go into the open after the fire commenced. This was probably a correct assumption, and if so, it lent substance to the Bulgarian contention that the fact of the corpse's position should be verified immediately. The selection of Scanagatta was probably the only choice. It would not interfere with the League's inquiry, and accordingly he approved.[51] He added that, as long as armed Greek and Bulgar troops faced each other at a distance of only thirty yards, incidents like this one would continue to take place. The first step, he thought, towards a real pacification of the area would be 'the creation of demilitarised frontier zones in the Balkans'.[52]

Howard Smith submitted that Stevenson deserved 'great credit' for his action. He had had to make up his mind quickly and it was clear that he had carried his colleague in Sofia with him. The clearing up of the position of the Greek corpse would be important for the League when it had to make up its mind as to the origin of the incident. He therefore suggested that Lampson, who had accompanied Chamberlain to Paris, approve Stevenson's initiative directly from the French capital.[53]

Leone's decision to collaborate with Stevenson and Dard, despite his lack of instructions, is understandable in the light of the information that had come into his possession earlier that day. Like Stevenson, he too had ascertained that the situation at the frontier was deteriorating and had consequently flashed this news to Rome before Stevenson's visit to the Italian Legation. According to Leone's communication to Rome, both the Bulgarian Foreign Ministry and the General Staff early that morning had informed him that Greek forces were still holding all positions and maintaining their artillery fire. Minkoff reassured him that the Bulgarian military continued their passive attitude. Nevertheless Leone reported to the Italian Foreign Ministry that information had come to his attention that further Bulgarian reinforcements were on their way to the place of

[51] Minute by C.B., 26 Oct. 1925. File 13309, FO/371/10672, PRO.
[52] Minute by C.H.B., 26 Oct. 1925. File 13309, FO/371/10672, PRO.
[53] Minute by C. Howard Smith, 26 Oct. 1925. File 13309, FO/371/10672, PRO. Also C.H.S. to Lampson, 26 Oct. 1925. File 13309, FO/371/10672, PRO.

conflict. He therefore thought it necessary to act at Athens with the greatest speed, 'since the situation could deteriorate from one moment to the next'.[54]

Leone's subsequent visit to Kalfoff, accompanied by Stevenson and Dard, and the British chargé's initiative in this move, was quickly reported to Athens by the ever-watchful Greek chargé, Rosetti.[55] The substance of this interview and Dard's communication to Briand, and the suggestion that Scanagatta proceed to the frontier as the neutral observer desired by Kalfoff was, of course, communicated by Leone to Rome.[56]

Late that evening, 25 October, in a conversation with Leone, Dard opined that in case the conflict worsened the League of Nations would be in a position to exert 'pressure' on Greece by 'granting the mandate to a Great Power of blockading an Aegean port', or perhaps an island like Mytilene. As to the Bulgars, Yugoslavia or Rumania could be entrusted to occupy some 'important point of Bulgarian territory'. However, no penetration by Yugoslavia in the direction of Salonika was envisaged.[57]

Somewhat analogous sentiments were expressed by Stevenson, who informed his American colleague 'that should the Greeks refuse the arbitration of the League his Government stood ready to utilize their Mediterranean Fleet in order to bring them to their senses'. He felt that if no definite understanding could be quickly arrived at, 'all the work of the Locarno Conference would appear futile, and Britain had no idea of allowing that to take place'.[58]

Fortunately for Athens, these threats never evolved into physical actions, even though the following day the League Council convened and the pressure on Athens increased. This time, however, the pressures of the Great Powers were channelled through the League of Nations and disguised as the intended actions of the world organization. It was to these disguised pressures that Greece, as we shall now see, inevitably succumbed.

[54] Weill Schott [Leone] (Sofia) to Mussolini, 25 Oct. 1925. Italian Archives.
[55] Rosetti (Sofia) to the F.Min., no. 1819, 26 Oct. 1925. Greek Archives.
[56] Weill Schott [Leone] (Sofia) to Mussolini, 25 Oct. 1925. Italian Archives.
[57] Weill Schott [Leone] (Sofia) to Mussolini, 26 Oct. 1925. Italian Archives.
[58] Cable (Sofia) to the Dept. of State, 26 Oct. 1925. File 768.74/232, Record Group 59, NA.

V

COERCION THROUGH THE LEAGUE OF NATIONS

The Council Convenes
THE Council's first meeting to deal with the incident was held, as scheduled, in Paris on Monday, 26 October, at 6 p.m. The meeting was public. As Acting President of the League Council, Briand dominated the discussions. His actions and the convening of the Council were warmly commended by the Spanish representative, José Martin Quiñones de León, and by Chamberlain. Briand's proposal was that the Council should hear from the Greek and Bulgarian representatives what actions their respective governments were taking 'with regard to the cessation of hostilities and the withdrawal of troops' and what was the present situation at the frontier.

The reply of the Bulgarian representative, the minister in Paris, Bogdan Marfoff, was that 'at no moment and at no point has Greek territory been invaded or occupied' by Bulgar forces. Furthermore, Sofia was ready to submit to an inquiry on this point.

Greece's representative was also its minister in Paris. Carapanos was in an unenviable position. Though his government agreed without hesitation to comply with Briand's request to Athens to evacuate Bulgarian territory, it would only do so 'as soon as the Bulgarians have quitted Greek territory'—a major qualification.

At this point Briand called a private meeting of the Council to examine the situation, Chamberlain being invited to act as *rapporteur*. Briand thought that the Council members, excluding the Greek and Bulgarian representatives, would desire to discuss the matter among themselves and therefore hoped that Carapanos and Marfoff would permit the Council members to do so. Accordingly the Greek and Bulgarian representatives retired from the room. After an exchange of views between the different delegations, Carapanos and Marfoff were invited to the Council's private session, at which a draft resolution drawn up by Chamberlain was approved. The same resolution was later adopted in the public meeting of the Council which immediately followed.

Before presenting the resolution to the Council, Chamberlain made some remarks on the situation that had developed. A border incident, he observed, had erupted between two League members, both of whom had assumed the obligations of the League's Covenant. In particular he pointed out the obligations of Articles 10 and 12 of the Covenant. Incidents such as the present one, which had caused the convening of the League Council, had in the past had very serious consequences, when there was no international machinery like that of the League for peacefully settling disputes and securing justice for both sides. Chamberlain thought it would be intolerable—indeed, an affront to civilized society—if the League's machinery and the Council's good offices were not immediately used, and the frontier incident was allowed to lead to warlike actions, instead of being submitted quickly to the League Council for peaceful and friendly settlement by the countries concerned. The Council would always be concerned for the honour and for the safety and security of the two Balkan states.

The resolution that Chamberlain now offered the Council began by approving Briand's prior communication to both countries. However, the Council was not satisfied that military operations had ceased and that the troops had been withdrawn behind their respective national frontiers. It therefore requested Carapanos and Marfoff to inform the Council within twenty-four hours that unconditional orders had been given to their forces to 'withdraw behind their respective national frontiers'. Within sixty hours all forces were to be withdrawn within their own frontiers, all hostilities to have ceased and all troops to have been warned that resumption of firing would be severely punished.

To assist the Council and the two states, the governments of London, Paris, and Rome were requested to direct their military personnel who were within reach to proceed quickly to the area of conflict and report directly to the League Council as soon as the troops of both states had been withdrawn and hostilities had ceased. Lastly, Athens and Sofia were requested to extend to these officers all the facilities they would require for the execution of their mission.

Asked by Briand whether he had any objections to raise, Marfoff replied that he was authorized to declare that Sofia was ready to comply with the terms of the resolution passed. Carapanos unfortunately was not in so secure a position as his Bulgarian colleague. Though he had no objections to the terms of the resolution, he was bound to forward the terms to Athens, 'which would, he was convinced, comply with them'.

Before closing the meeting, Chamberlain made the point, to which his Council colleagues agreed, that the time limit stipulated in the resolution should begin from the present session.

To cover all eventualities Briand made it clear to both Carapanos and Marfoff that the essential point was to stop the firing, which meant that the troops, upon their withdrawal across the frontier, had to cease 'all acts of hostility'.[1] After the Council adjourned, Carapanos sent an urgent telegram to Athens requesting that immediate instructions be forwarded to him so that he would be in a position to 'reply within [the] time [limit] allowed'.[2]

That day in London, the arrival of Kalfoff's appeal to Sir Eric Drummond, the League's Secretary-General, against Greece's continuing military operations prompted Bateman to minute that it was becoming as clear as day that the advance of the Greeks into Bulgaria had been undertaken with some other motive than merely dislodging the Bulgars from two frontier posts in Greek territory— as the Greeks had alleged. Bateman felt that a few well-directed shells would have effected all that was necessary in that direction; but had the Bulgars been thus dislodged, Athens would have had no excuse for an advance into Bulgaria; they had therefore let the Bulgars occupy these frontier posts.

Bateman presumed that if the Greeks remained recalcitrant, the League would deal with them in one of the following ways: either they would threaten a demonstration by the Allied fleet at Piraeus, Athens's adjacent seaport; or they would threaten to allow Bulgaria to arm in self-defence. The latter, he noted, 'would frighten the life out of [General] Pangalos'. Another official in the Foreign Office minuted that he was afraid Bateman's second proposal would bring in the Yugoslavs on the Greek side, but anyhow assumed that the League's first act would be to order an inquiry.[3]

There was also news from Belgrade. According to Kennard, the

[1] League of Nations, *Official Journal*, 6th year, 1925, pp. 1697–1700.
[2] Carapanos (Paris) to the F.Min., no. 4903, 26 Oct. 1925. French Text. Greek Archives.
[3] Minute by C.H.B. and an attached minute with an illegible signature, 26 Oct. 1925. File 13309, FO/371/10672, PRO.

news from the frontier was that firing had continued throughout the night. The Yugoslav military attaché in Sofia had reported that 10,000 komitadjis were involved in the fighting, which was growing in intensity, as the Greeks were determined to occupy the post where the body of the dead Greek soldier lay. The Greek Minister in Belgrade, Spyridion Polychroniadis, discussing the question of responsibility for the incident, stated that in his opinion it would have been easy for the Bulgars to have dragged the body of the Greek soldier across the frontier line. Bateman's reaction to this communication was to minute that he imagined the Greek Minister in Belgrade had never been under fire. If Polychroniadis had, he would have been less likely to have made such a statement to Kennard. If it were indeed true, as reported by the Yugoslav military attaché in Sofia, that 10,000 komitadjis were involved in the fighting, then the Greeks might 'have reason to regret their rashness'.[4]

In a follow-up message, Kennard explained that Polychroniadis had been impressed by the anti-Greek tone of the Yugoslav press. Kennard had observed to the Greek Minister that this was hardly unexpected, and feared that similar views might be found elsewhere. The British Minister, 'speaking personally and frankly', thought that Polychroniadis had made an error in not having visited the Yugoslav Foreign Ministry since the inception of the incident, in view of the fact that his Bulgarian colleague had been there often. To this observation the Greek Minister admitted that this was perhaps so. He then suggested to Kennard that the Yugoslavs desired to play the role of arbiters. His British colleague did not agree, pointing out that since the eruption of the incident the Yugoslavs had taken a neutral stance and had stated their intention of leaving the question 'in the hands of the Great Powers'. The Greek Minister, Kennard concluded, seemed 'generally to feel [that the] Greek Government ha[d] acted foolishly and [that] military Gov[ernmen]ts [were] a mistake'.[5]

[4] Kennard (Belgrade) to the F.O., no. 144, 26 Oct. 1925, and the attached minute by C.H.B., File 13309, FO/371/10672, PRO.
[5] Belgrade to Athens, addressed to the F.O., no. 145, repeated to Sofia, 2[6] Oct. 1925. File 953, FO/286/916, PRO.
The anti-Greek atmosphere to be found in Belgrade had been reported to Athens by Polychroniadis before he had called on Kennard. (Polychroniadis (Belgrade) to the F.Min., no. 1702, 24 Oct. 1925; Polychroniadis (Belgrade) to the F.Min., no. 1702, 25 Oct. 1925; Polychroniadis (Belgrade) to the F.Min., no. 1704, 25 Oct. 1925. French Texts. Greek Archives.)

In Sofia that same day, 26 October, it was reported that the Greek bombardment continued, though it was less severe than the day before. The burning by the Greeks of a village recently constructed by Bulgarian refugees from Greek Macedonia caused great indignation, which was in no way lessened by the news of a somewhat provocative Greek note handed to Kalfoff the night before by the Greek chargé, Rosetti, on instructions from Athens. The note stated that a senior Greek officer had been dispatched to the frontier and had established beyond question that, not only were the Bulgars in the wrong in the original incident, but they were still occupying a strip of Greek territory varying in depth from five to fifty metres. Nevertheless the atmosphere in the Bulgarian capital was generally somewhat better than the day before, owing, Stevenson believed, primarily to the fact that no further advance by the Greek military had been reported. Moreover, Stevenson was informed by a reliable source of the good effect produced by the joint action he had initiated, after consultation with his French and Italian colleagues. Although he and his colleagues had not succeeded in bringing about the immediate withdrawal of the Bulgarian forces from the frontier, as they had hoped, owing to the attitude of the Italian chargé, Leone, their action had not been 'altogether fruitless'.[6]

Reading Stevenson's report at the Foreign Office on the following day, 27 October, Bateman minuted that the Greeks would 'have to be taken seriously to task' for their continual shelling and arson. The bombardment had apparently continued long after the Council's meeting of the previous night, when the Council had requested that orders be dispatched within twenty-four hours for both sides to withdraw behind their own frontiers. To Bateman this connoted the Council's will that the hostilities come to an end. The Greeks did not appear to be carrying out the Council's wishes.

Polychroniadis did not call on the Yugoslav Foreign Minister, Ninčić, until 27 October, at which point Ninčić informed him that Belgrade would assume a strictly neutral attitude in the present question. (Polychroniadis (Belgrade) to the F.Min., no. 1718, 27 Oct. 1925. French Text. Greek Archives.) However, the Yugoslav attitude had been communicated to Athens some days before, thanks to Caclamanos in London, who quoted the statements of the Under-Secretary of the Yugoslav Foreign Ministry given in an interview with a British journalist. (Caclamanos (London) to the F. Min., no. 2831, 24 Oct. 1925. Greek Archives.)

[6] Stevenson (Sofia) to the F.O., no. 93, 26 Oct. 1925. File 13309, FO/371/10672, PRO; Stevenson (Sofia) to Chamberlain, no. 231, 28 Oct. 1925. File 13309, FO/371/10673, PRO.

The burning of the village, Bateman observed, had taken place on Sunday, some hours after Athens had been warned by Briand of its obligations under Article 12 of the Covenant. Should not the Council be requested, he noted, to send a sharp note immediately, saying that Greece was 'running a grave risk of being put out of court by her monstrous behaviour', and that unless the shelling ceased forthwith, the Council would take such action as it thought 'fit to enforce a cessation of hostilities'.[7]

When the League Council convened in Paris that day, 27 October, attempts to solve the dispute were also being undertaken in the Greek and Bulgarian capitals by the Rumanian Government. At the beginning of the incident, it had been reported to London that the Rumanian Foreign Minister, John Duca, had urged the Greeks in the interests of peace to avoid disturbing the tranquillity of the Balkans and to exercise moderation towards the Bulgars. He had expressed the opinion that reference to the League would be the most reasonable course and had also repeated these views to the Bulgarian chargé d'affaires in Bucharest. Subsequently, when the Greek Minister in Bucharest, Constantine Collas, gave Duca a copy of Greece's ultimatum to Bulgaria and had informed him that Athens was opposed to referring the matter to the League, Duca repeated his view that peace must be maintained and reference of the issue to the League would be the best way of ensuring it. Accordingly he requested Collas to communicate his view to the Athens government.[8]

Bateman, when this report arrived in the Foreign Office on 26 October, thought that it was good advice. But General Pangalos, he noted, had paid little attention to British advice until it became apparent that the League of Nations meant business. It seemed

[7] Minute by C. H. Bateman, 27 Oct. 1925. File 13309, FO/371/10672, PRO. At about this time Cheetham asked the Foreign Office from Athens whether it was conceivable that the komitadjis had started the present trouble in order to embarrass the government in Sofia. He also pointed to increasing Bolshevik influence in Bulgaria. (Cheetham (Athens) to the F.O., no. 173, 26 Oct. 1925. File 13309, FO/371/10673, PRO.) Bateman's reaction was negative. He did not believe that the komitadjis were interested in toppling the government in Sofia. He also dismissed the possibility that the Bolsheviks knew anything about the present situation. (Minute by C. H. Bateman, 27 Oct. 1925. File 13309, FO/371/10673, PRO.)

[8] Dering (Bucharest) to the F.O., no. 74, 24 Oct. 1925. File 13309, FO/371/10672, PRO. Also Savona (Bucharest) to Mussolini, 26 Oct. 1925. Italian Archives.

hardly likely to Bateman that Pangalos would pay greater attention to Rumania.[9]

In fact, Bateman was proved wrong. As requested by the Rumanian Foreign Minister, Collas informed Athens that the Rumanian Government desired the incident to be settled peacefully and as quickly as possible in order that the 'peace of the Balkans may not be troubled'.[10] The Secretary-General of the Rumanian Foreign Ministry subsequently outlined to Collas the attitude and opinions of the Rumanian Government on this question. According to the Foreign Ministry's Secretary-General, the frontier incident 'had not been dictated by [Bulgarian] sentiments of enmity' towards Greece. He felt certain that Sofia 'had no interest in troubling the peace' at the very moment it was striving to consolidate its own position. For these reasons, Bucharest, anxious that all incidents occurring in the Balkans be settled in a friendly manner so that the peace might not be disturbed, had 'given instructions to its Ministers at Sofia and at Athens to mediate before the respective Governments in order to make known [the] point of view [of the] Rumanian Government and to arrive [at a] pacific settlement of the frontier incident'.[11]

With this end in mind, the Rumanian Minister in Athens, Langa Rascano, had approached the Greek Government on the morning of 26 October. The three propositions tendered by Rascano to General Pangalos, the Prime Minister, and Caftanzoglou, the Foreign Ministry's Secretary-General, were accepted with alacrity. They were also communicated to the Bulgarian chargé, Dantcheff as well as to Bucharest and Paris.

Rascano's proposals stipulated that a Greek and a Bulgarian staff officer proceed on the following day at four in the afternoon to Demir-Kapu to establish the Greek frontier guards at their respective posts. This action accomplished, the Greek forces occupying Bulgarian territory would begin their withdrawal into Greek territory as quickly as possible. Finally, during the withdrawal of the Greek forces, the Bulgarian military facing them would not advance

---

[9] Minute by C.H.B., 26 Oct. 1925. File 13309, FO/371/10672, PRO.
[10] Collas (Bucharest) to the F.Min., no. 1809, 24 Oct. 1925. French Text. Greek Archives.
[11] Collas (Bucharest) to the F.Min., no. 1359, 27 Oct. 1925. French Text. Greek Archives. Also Savona (Bucharest) to Mussolini, 28 Oct. 1925. Italian Archives.

until the Greek forces had crossed the frontier.[12] Cheetham's observation to the Foreign Office was that his Rumanian colleague, Rascano, had, like himself, found during these negotiations 'great difficulty', in convincing Pangalos—for all intents and purposes the Greek Government—of 'the real dangers of the situation'.[13] In Sofia, Stevenson expressed the fear that without the presence of neutral observers at the frontier there was always a danger that 'a further incident might take place'[14] during the meeting of the Greek and Bulgarian staff officers.

In Sofia, attempts to solve the dispute were furthered by the Turkish Government, which wanted to know whether there was a possibility of arranging the incident 'by a mixed commission of inquiry'. Kalfoff's reply was that since the League Council was considering the issue, the Bulgarian Government found it impossible to enter into direct negotiations with the Greek Government. A similar reply was transmitted by Minkoff to the Rumanian Minister, who had inquired whether Rascano in Athens could not intervene to help in settling the dispute. However, since Rascano had already made his overtures and the Greek Government had dispatched a senior officer to Demir-Kapu to effect a meeting with a Bulgarian officer, Sofia, out of courtesy, on 27 October ordered a senior Bulgarian officer, Colonel Zlateff, to proceed to the border also. In the presence of foreign journalists, Colonel Zlateff made it clear to his Greek counterpart that he could not negotiate with him, since the whole question was in the hands of the League Council and would be resolved by that body.[15] The Rumanian overtures were thus unsuccessful.

[12] Text. *Le Messager d'Athènes*, 27 Oct. 1925, p. 4; France. Ministère des Affaires Étrangères, *Bulletin Périodique de la Presse Grecque*, no. 84, p. 11.
[13] Athens to the F.O., no. 174, 27 Oct. 1925. File 953, FO/286/916, PRO.
[14] Sofia to Athens, addressed to the F.O., no. 95, repeated to Belgrade, Bucharest, Constantinople, Paris, and Rome, 27 Oct. 1925. File 953, FO/286/916, PRO; Stevenson (Sofia) to Chamberlain, no. 231, 28 Oct. 1925. File 13309, FO/371/10673, PRO.
[15] Ministère des Affaires Étrangères (Bulgarie), Récapitulation des événments concernant l'incident gréco-bulgare de Demir-Kapia jusqu'au moment de l'intervention du Conseil de la Société des Nations. Political 1925, League of Nations Archives. Also Weill Schott [Leone] (Sofia) to Mussolini, 28 Oct. 1925. Italian Archives; Stevenson (Sofia) to Chamberlain, no. 231, 28 Oct. 1925. File 13309, FO/371/10673, PRO.
As early as 24 October, the Greek Minister in Angora (Ankara), following a conversation with the Turkish Foreign Minister, reported to Athens that it was his impression that the Foreign Minister desired to act as an 'intermediary' in the dispute. The Turkish overtures to Sofia several days later, therefore, could

Discussions of Sanctions

The disclosure of Rumania's endeavours by Carapanos at the Council's Tuesday morning session, 27 October, prompted Briand to observe that the situation had not changed in any way, and he hoped that Athens would reply to the Council's communication of the previous day. He noted that, while agreeing with the Rumanian Government, Greece 'had made certain reservations which appeared to attach conditions and which were in contradiction to the text of the decision of the Council'. Briand was undoubtedly referring to the phrase in Hadjikyriakos's telegram to Carapanos that Greece had stipulated 'as a *sine quâ non* that it [would] evacuate Bulgarian territory only after the Bulgarians had retreated from the Greek post [of] Demir-Kapu which they continued to occupy'.

In reply, Carapanos observed that an agreement had been concluded between the two interested parties, to which conditions had been added. However, these conditions were agreed to by both sides. Therefore, they 'were not conditions in the precise sense of the word, but rather methods proposed for carrying out the evacuation'. Briand had no objection to a bilateral agreement. But the problem at the moment, regardless of any desire to come to an agreement, was that the firing continued. As long as this situation persisted, nothing could be achieved. It was only to be hoped that later news would prove 'entirely satisfactory'. In the meantime he invited statements from both Marfoff and Carapanos.

Marfoff's speech was merely a long recitation of the Bulgarian version of the events of the past week. Carapanaos's remarks which followed, dictated by instructions from Athens, were also merely a repetition of all previous Greek arguments. In one respect, however, this proved to be of greater interest: Carapanos insisted that on the Greek side there had not been 'any hostile act "likely to lead to a rupture" within the terms of Article 12 of the Covenant'. This argument, though questionable at first glance, appears on closer examination to be valid. Certainly, diplomatic relations between the Greeks and the Bulgars had not been severed, and Carapanos, if he had wanted to, could have pointed to the Corfu Incident of two years earlier where an analogous situation had developed between Greece and Italy and yet relations had continued undisturbed.

---

have come as no surprise to the Greek Foreign Ministry. (Argyropoulos (Angora) to the F.Min., no. 3731, 24 Oct. 1925. Greek Archives.)

When Carapanos finished his presentation, Briand asked if any-one on the Council wished to make any observations. Chamberlain asked Carapanos to what depth the Greek Army had penetrated into Bulgaria, and conversely how deep the Bulgarians had pene-trated into Greece. His own information, Chamberlain added, was that Athens had presented a note to Sofia alleging that the Bul-garian military had penetrated into Greek territory to a depth vary-ing from five to fifty metres. Carapanos replied that he thought the Bulgarian penetration was from 400 to 500 metres, in relation to the two Greek frontier posts. The purpose of the flanking move-ment carried out by the Greek Army was to avoid a frontal assault, which would have caused losses to both sides. The depth of the Greek penetration into Bulgaria could not be exactly determined. Owing to the flanking movement the Bulgarian territory occupied constituted a considerable area. Chamberlain noted that the Bul-garian penetration of Greek territory extended to 500 metres. How many kilometres had the Greeks penetrated into Bulgaria? Carapanos replied that Greek penetration amounted to nearly eight kilometres. At this point Marfoff relayed to the Council the proposal made by the Allied representatives in Sofia to Kalfoff to send a representative to the frontier to ascertain exactly where the body of the slain Greek soldier was to be found, a proposal which Kalfoff had conditionally accepted, providing the League of Nations approved of it also.[16]   .

Reading the minutes of this meeting in London, Bateman wrote that Marfoff's and Carapanos's statements were merely a 'rehash of the confused and contradictory stories' which had already reached London. They were primarily concerned with the origins of the incident. This, however, was not the important point at the present moment. Responsibility for the incident could be fixed at a later date. What the Council had to do quickly was to force the Greeks and the Bulgars to stop hostilities and withdraw behind their own lines. He noted that Chamberlain's remark 'comparing the distances of penetration on each side was very pointed'.[17]

On the same day, 27 October, as the League Council convened

---

[16] League of Nations, *Official Journal*, 6th year, 1925, pp. 1700–7. Carapanos's orders had been sent on 25 October, but probably arrived in time to be used only for the Council session of 27 October. Greek F.Min. to the Greek Legation in Paris, no. 15045, 25 Oct. 1925. Greek Archives.

[17] Minute by C. H. Bateman, attached to the Council's minutes of 27 Oct. 1925. File 13309, FO/371/10672, PRO.

in Paris, Howard Smith of the Foreign Office's Central Department wrote to his chief, Miles W. Lampson, who had accompanied Chamberlain to Paris. He referred to a dispatch that Stevenson had sent several days before which seemed to Howard Smith 'to point to one of the real causes of these frontier difficulties between the two countries'. From Stevenson's dispatch, it appeared that some places along the Greek-Bulgar border frontier posts were no more than thirty yards apart. This meant that armed and volatile Greeks were literally looking down every day at loaded Bulgarian rifle barrels. What was more natural than that, out of boredom perhaps, someone would occasionally fire a round off at such short range that it would be impossible to miss the target? The fun would then begin, and so long as this proximity existed between the frontier posts, it would continue. It had occurred to the Foreign Office, Howard Smith continued, that when the Council had overcome the present difficulties, it might be wise for it to consider whether the prevention of future incidents was not better than their subsequent cure, and to safeguard against future incidents by removing what appeared to be the main cause of the present one.

It was Howard Smith's argument that, under Article 11 of the League Covenant, it was within the Council's competence to deal with the question of the proximity of the Greek-Bulgar frontier posts by classifying the matter as a circumstance which threatened world peace. Moreover, since the League Council had been convened to deal with an actual breach of the peace in which this question was involved, it appeared an opportune moment to deal with it. He therefore inquired how it would be for Great Britain to insist on using its 'friendly right' to bring the frontier situation to the Council's notice? It might suggest that since the present proximity of the frontier posts caused 'irritation and friction', the Council should insist that they be separated by a distance of 2,000 yards, twice the maximum distance of effective rifle fire. The actual frontier line could run down the centre, between the line of the frontier posts, about 1,000 yards from each.

It was naturally impossible to think in terms of fully fledged frontier arrangements in the Balkans along the lines agreed upon at Locarno. The time was not ripe for it; but London could start things off by arranging for a miniature demilitarized zone between Greece and Bulgaria, and the League Council could declare that any soldier in uniform found within the zone 'would be out of bounds and liable to be shot'. Any shooting could not then be considered as a provocative act by either side, because if a soldier were shot he would have had to be within range and thus 'more or less on forbidden ground'. This was, of course, only a suggestion and there were many difficulties which soon became apparent. For example, what arrangements would night patrols require? How would they deal with encroaching komitadjis, etc.? How could peasants situated between the lines be protected? These problems, Howard Smith commented, would be for the Council to iron out, if Lampson thought it worth while to suggest this plan.

All this, he divulged, was 'Bateman's brain-wave'. The Assistant Under-Secretary, Tyrrell, agreed completely to have this proposal put before him. Howard Smith was sure that there was much to be said for it, especially in view of the fact, reported in recent communications, that the Greeks were maintaining that the Bulgarians were in the wrong because they were five metres inside Greek territory! The close proximity of the Greek and Bulgar posts could 'be reduced to an absurdity, because of the axiom that a point has position but no magnitude, both Greek and Bulgar blockhouses might be in the same spot'![18]

In his report to Athens describing the day's events, Carapanos found it necessary to stress that the 'atmosphere' at the Council was not friendly towards Greece's position. He again begged for instructions, warning that the time limit stipulated by the Council on the previous day would elapse that evening. In conclusion, he felt obliged to emphasize the 'important consequences' that might develop, should Athens either reject the Council's request or reply to it tardily.[19]

If Carapanos had known of the private and informal meeting of the Council members held at 5 p.m. that afternoon, his report to Athens would perhaps have been even more pressing. At this meeting, Vittorio Scialoja, Italy's Council representative, asked his colleagues to consider what action they could take in the dispute under Article 16 of the Covenant—the article dealing with the imposition of sanctions upon an aggressor state. Replying, the Secretary-General, Sir Eric Drummond, pointed out that the League Assembly had proposed in 1921 that under Article 16, the first

[18] Howard Smith to Lampson, 27 Oct. 1925. File 13309, FO/371/10672, PRO.
[19] Carapanos (Paris) to the F.Min., no. 4915, 27 Oct. 1925. Greek Archives.

action should be the withdrawal of diplomatic representatives. Briand contended that the mere withdrawal of diplomatic representatives would appear 'too feeble' a move. As he expressed it, 'if the leak were not stopped up at once, there might be a flood'. To Briand, Rumanian intervention was merely an attempt 'to mask the League's action'. If Greece's attitude were to continue, 'it was essential for the Council to act at once and to act strongly'. Though Chamberlain agreed that at the proper moment the Council should act with vigour and dispatch, he felt it should do so according to the Covenant.

As to specific details, Scialoja asked whether economic or military measures should be applied. With Greece's extended coast line and innumerable islands in mind, his own inclination was undoubtedly towards the latter alternative, in the form a of naval demonstration; this, he thought, would be the most effective.

Briand felt that the objection to a blockade was that it would affect both innocent and guilty. However, if the Council did act under Article 16 of the Covenant, its action had to be quick, strong and decisive. He noted that one of the greatest arguments against the world organization was that its enforcement machinery was slow and clumsy. Sir Austen was not moved by his colleagues' arguments, however. He believed that a Greek decision rejecting the Council's overtures would be impossible. At any rate, if there were a rejection, he felt that a blockade was an unnecessarily large action in such a situation. Meanwhile, he thought it unnecessary to take a decision. After some closing remarks by Briand, the Council members agreed, at least for the moment, that they would make no moves with regard to possible action under Article 16 of the Covenant.[20]

If Greece refused to cease her military operations and to withdraw her army from Bulgaria, Chamberlain informed London, the League Council was strongly in favour of recommending the immediate withdrawal of chiefs of diplomatic missions in Athens, to be followed, if Greece continued recalcitrant, by an immediate naval demonstration at Athens's adjacent seaport city of Piraeus. According to Chamberlain, it was the Council's unanimous feel-

[20] Record of [a] Private Informal Meeting of Members of [the] Council, held on 27 Oct. at 5 p.m. Political 1925, League of Nations Archives. A good synopsis of the meeting was sent to Rome. (Scialoja (Paris) to Mussolini, 27 Oct. 1925. Italian Archives. Also Carapanos (Paris) to the F.Min., no. 4976, 30 Oct. 1925. Greek Archives.)

ing that the situation was fraught with danger. It was not certain that the Athens government could withdraw its army from Bulgaria 'without [the] support given by external pressure'. Furthermore, the Council feared complications from komitadjis in the event of a delay, and was apprehensive lest the Turks or Yugoslavs should intervene. It was felt by the Council that in Greece's case a naval demonstration would 'be at once more rapidly effective and less disturbing than [the] adoption of general economic sanctions contemplated by the [League's] covenant'.

Chamberlain proposed to support such a recommendation if the circumstances called for it, but he thought it 'extremely improbable' that Athens would refuse the Council's request. However, if this were to happen, the 'whole position of the Council and [the] effectiveness of the [League] covenant as [a] means of preventing war [would] be at stake and action [would] be necessary'. On the other hand, success by the League Council in this case would 'act as [a] great deterrent to warlike action in case of any other frontier dispute'.[21]

Bateman's minute to this communication was that things had been working up to this action for the past several days. Greece had done its best to put itself 'out of court', owing to the fact that Greece's dictator, General Pangalos, did not 'realize his own danger'.[22] Since the message arrived while the Cabinet was sitting, it was immediately sent over to them for consideration.[23] After discussion it was agreed that the Prime Minister, Stanley Baldwin, was to inform Chamberlain that the Cabinet agreed to his proposal, but they, of course, did so 'on the assumption that any [naval] demonstration against Greece would be a joint one'.[24]

Summoned to the Prime Minister's office, Howard Smith of the Central Department was told of the Cabinet's decision to concur with Chamberlain's recommendation and to support the proposal 'if necessary provided that the [naval] demonstration was not made by British ships alone'. It was essential, according to Baldwin, that the French and the Italians shared in any naval demonstration or blockade of the Greek coast, otherwise these two states would, if

---

[21] Crewe (Paris) to the F.O., no. 377, 27 Oct. 1925. File 13309, FO/371/10672, PRO.

[22] Minute by C.H.B., 28 Oct. 1925. File 13309, FO/371/10672, PRO.

[23] Minute by C. Howard Smith, 28 Oct. 1925. File 13309, FO/371/10672, PRO.

[24] A meeting of the British Cabinet, 28 Oct. 1925. File CAB/23/51, PRO.

Britain undertook to act alone, 'make capital out of it', in order to oust Great Britain further 'from trade with Greece'.[25]

The Cabinet's concurrence was immediately dispatched to Chamberlain in Paris, supporting his recommendation for a naval demonstration against the Greeks if this proved necessary, provided that the demonstration was 'not carried out by British ships only'. The Cabinet, Chamberlain was informed, considered 'it essential that all available naval powers should take part, in order to avoid any power being tempted to exploit any such measures for selfish purposes'.[26] The possibility, however, of a naval demonstration against the Greeks, led the League Secretariat to engage in 'unofficial discussions as to the form, and legal authority, under which, if the need arose, such action should be taken'.[27] These discussions in the end proved to be unnecessary. For, as Chamberlain had prophesied, the Greeks soon gave in to Council pressure.

Athens's surrender took place at the morning session of the Council, on Wednesday, 28 October. The Bulgarian representative, Marfoff, as was to be expected, communicated a telegram he had received from Sofia the previous day agreeing to the Council's resolution. According to Kalfoff's message, 'strict orders' had been given to the Bulgarian military to cease all military action 'either within Bulgarian territory or along the frontier'. At the same time, renewed orders had been sent to the Bulgarian Army to 'withdraw immediately any Bulgarian troops which may be on Greek territory'.

Diplomatically isolated and with the threat of sanctions looming on the horizon, the Greek Government was in no position to resist. Thus, according to Carapanos, the government in Athens, after receipt of the Council's resolution, had only repeated and confirmed its previous instructions to the Greek military to evacuate Bulgarian territory. These orders had been given earlier in conforming with the Rumanian offer of mediation communicated to the League previously.

In order to assure himself that there was no misunderstanding,

---

[25] Minute by C. Howard Smith, 28 Oct. 1925. File 13309, FO/371/10672, PRO.

[26] F.O. to Crewe, no. 304, 28 Oct. 1925. File 13309, FO/371/10672, PRO.

[27] Memorandum by J. A. S[alter] entitled, The Greco-Bulgar Incident 'Sanctions', dated 9 Nov. 1925. Political 1925, League of Nations Archives. Salter's interesting memorandum and a critique by the Dutch Director of the Secretariat's Legal Section, Dr. Joost Adrian van Hamel, as well as a covering note by the Secretary-General, Sir Eric Drummond, are to be found as Appendices A, B, and C.

Briand turned and asked Carapanos whether this meant 'that the Greek Government had given orders that all hostilities should cease'. Carapanos replied in the affirmative. Did the telegram also imply, Briand asked, that Athens would facilitate the task of the officers proceeding to the area of conflict? Undoubtedly, responded the Greek representative. Noting with satisfaction that the first part of the Council's resolution had been accepted by both Greece and Bulgaria, Briand observed that the second part of the resolution 'allowed a period of 60 hours within which the orders had to be not only issued but also carried out'. He hoped that by the next day all these movements would be completed, and desired to make one observation: he understood Carapanos to have indicated that all these incidents would not have occurred if Greece had not been obliged to take immediate steps for 'its legitimate defence and protection'. It was essential that such thoughts should not develop in the minds of nations which were also League members, and 'become a kind of jurisprudence, for it would be extremely dangerous'. With the excuse of 'legitimate defence', disputes might develop which, though limited in extent, could be most unfortunate because of the damage they might entail. These disputes, once they had erupted, might assume such proportions that the party which had initiated them as 'legitimate defence' would no longer be able to control them. The League, through the Council and the peaceful methods at its disposal, offered to states the means of avoiding such situations. One had only to apply to the League Council. The criticisms against the League machinery, that it was cumbersome and slow in emergency situations, were unjustified. It had been proved that a state which appealed to the world organization, when it felt threatened, could be sure that the League Council would be ready to undertake the task of conciliation. With these sentiments Sir Austen Chamberlain and other members of the Council concurred.[28]

Doubtless fearing that the second part of the Council's resolution might not be executed, Carapanos, in an urgent and detailed message to Athens describing the day's events, warned that in such a situation the League might 'adopt against Greece Article 16 [of the] Covenant calling for [a] complete economic blockade [of the] country'.[29]

In London, when Bateman had read the minutes of this Council

---

[28] League of Nations, *Official Journal*, 6th year, 1925, pp. 1707–10.
[29] Carapanos (Paris) to the F.Min., no. 4930, 28 Oct. 1925. Greek Archives.

session, he asked whether Briand's remarks about the action of a state called upon suddenly to defend itself were not a 'little risky and illogical'. Bateman correctly pointed out that the Locarno Treaty 'clearly envisaged the case where a country could legitimately take up arms in defence without first appealing to the League'. Howard Smith minuted that 'unprovoked aggression' could not, he thought, 'be defined, as it must always be a question of opinion'.[30]

Also dispatched from Paris to London that day, apart from the minutes of the Council meeting, was a reply by Lampson to the communication sent to him the previous day by Howard Smith containing Bateman's proposal for a demilitarized zone on the Greek-Bulgarian frontier.

'Great minds think alike', Lampson wrote, for Bateman's idea had, in fact, been raised at a private meeting of the Council some days before and had not been unfavourably received. The position that had now been reached in Paris was that a League Commission of Inquiry would proceed immediately to the Greek-Bulgarian frontier to report on what had occurred. Simultaneously the Commission was to make such recommendations as it thought necessary for the prevention of similar frontier incidents. The way was thus open for the Commission to concern itself with the question of a demilitarized zone. From the way the Paris discussions had proceeded, Lampson had little doubt that a hint would be dropped to the Commission that it might study the possibilities of a demilitarized zone on the Greek-Bulgarian frontier. In fact, Chamberlain had shown Howard Smith's letter to the League's Secretary-General, Drummond, during that day's Council session, so that the Director of the League's Secretariat was now familiar with Bateman's idea. Beyond that, no more could be done at present.

It was Lampson's opinion that the whole thing had gone very well up to the present. Both the Greeks and Bulgars had stated that morning, during the Council meeting, that the necessary orders for the withdrawal of the troops inside their respective frontiers had been issued within the twenty-four-hour time limit laid down by the Council. It now only remained for the military attachés to report that, during the sixty-hour time limit established by the

Council, these orders had been executed and both Greek and Bulgarian soil was free of all invaders.

He did not think that anything more successful could have been hoped for. Certainly, the events of the past week had justified the League's intervention. In all probability, if the League had not acted, a first-class conflagration would have erupted in the Balkans. It was quite evident from the messages arriving from the Balkans, which Howard Smith had forwarded to Chamberlain and Lampson in Paris, that the conflict would have spread and involved the whole area. It was a 'very good week's work', he concluded. In a postscript, Lampson noted that he had got Chamberlain to send Stevenson in Sofia a message of commendation for his excellent work. 'It was certainly well earned: *not* so Athens, in my opinion!'— a slap at Cheetham for his indecision and lack of drive in a moment of crisis.[31]

What followed was, to a large extent, an anticlimax. Heeding Carapanos's appeal, Hadjikyriakos informed the League on the following day, 29 October, that Athens, desiring to conform to the Council's decision, had 'repeated its definite orders' hastening the withdrawal of Greek forces towards the frontier, in spite of harassment by armed Bulgarian bands. Most important, it would 'neglect no steps to ensure that the [*sic*] Bulgarian territory is evacuated by the hour laid down'. The withdrawal of the Greeks before the time limit set down by the Council was confirmed by the Allied military attachés who had been dispatched to the frontier, as well as by the French Minister in Athens, Chambrun.

Chamberlain's report as the Council's *rapporteur* was that, since hostilities had been brought to an end, the facts and responsibilities for the incident and the appropriate indemnities and reparations, if any were due, must be decided. Furthermore means should be discovered to eliminate any future outbreak of this type, and he noted that both sides welcomed a Council inquiry into the matter also. He therefore proposed a Commission of Inquiry be established by the League Council, composed of the following: as President of the Commission, Sir Horace Rumbold, an experienced diplomat and the British Ambassador in Madrid, a French and an Italian military officer, and two civilians of Swedish and Dutch nationality. The commission would operate in both countries and would be

[31] Lampson to Howard Smith, 28 Oct. 1925. File 13309, FO/371/10672, PRO.

given every assistance by the governments in Athens and Sofia. To this proposal the Council agreed, the Greek and Bulgar representatives included.[32]

On the same day Stevenson informed the Foreign Office from Sofia that the Greeks had completed their evacuation of Bulgarian territory without incident. The Bulgars, he observed, did not propose to re-occupy their frontier posts for several days.[33] Pangalos, Cheetham heard, had stated that he had 'never believed' that Sofia was 'responsible for [the] present situation'. He did think, however, that it was the task of the Bulgarian Government to 'keep [the] comitadjis in order'.[34] This communication prompted Bateman to write that if Pangalos had '*never* believed' that the Bulgarian authorities 'were responsible', why did the Athens government 'allow things to get to the present pass'?

This comment might perhaps foreshadow Athens's 'defence of their unwarrantable action'. On the other hand, neither the League Council nor the British Foreign Office could 'overlook the continual dangers to peace caused by the existence and activities of Macedonian komitadji' on Bulgaria's Greek and Yugoslav frontiers. The Foreign Office knew that the Bulgarian authorities had time and again 'compromised themselves through their intimate relations with the Macedonian Revolutionary Organisation'.

Bateman therefore thought that this was 'a good opportunity for the Council to warn' the Bulgars that they would 'forfeit a good deal of present sympathy unless they cut adrift once and for all from this illegally constituted and wholly baneful body'. With this one stroke, one could please the Yugoslavs, appease the Greeks, strengthen those in Sofia working for the fall of the present government and its sycophantic supporters whose influence was harmful and who were 'hand in glove with the M[acedonian] R[evolutionary] O[rganization]'. He was going to suggest this to Lampson privately.[35]

Howard Smith in reply thought it was 'probably true that the komitadji [were] at the bottom of this [incident], as they [were] of practically every frontier dispute in the Balkans', and the action

[32] League of Nations, *Official Journal*, 6th year, 1925, pp. 1711–13.

[33] Stevenson (Sofia) to the F.O., no. 100, 29 Oct. 1925. File 13309, FO/371/10673, PRO.

[34] Cheetham (Athens) to the F.O., no. 177, 28 Oct. 1925. File 13309, FO/371/10672, PRO.

[35] Minute by C. H. Bateman, 29 Oct. 1925. File 13309, FO/371/10672, PRO.

Bateman proposed might have the desired results. Yet at the same time he did not see that the League Council could very well address the warning Bateman desired to Bulgaria at the present time. There were different versions of the origins of the present incident, and the League's first task was to bring an end to the hostilities and get the troops on both sides inside their own frontiers. This, it was hoped, would be accomplished that day and the League would then establish a commission of inquiry, under the presidency of Sir Horace Rumbold, to ascertain the causes of the incident and assess damages, etc. It would be the Rumbold commission which would decide whether a Bulgarian komitadji had fired the first shot, or whether the incident had, for some obscure reason, been started by the Greeks or by the Bulgarian Government. If in the end it was proved to be due to the komitadjis, the Bulgarian authorities would be responsible, since the komitadjis were Bulgarian subjects and they should control them. The League at its December meeting would then attack the Bulgars on 'their attitude towards this subversive organisation'; but to have the League do it now would undoubtedly give the impression of prejudging the question before the world organization, with the aid of an independent inquiry, was able to come to a conclusion as to the facts of the case.

At the same time the Foreign Office had always known that the present Bulgarian Government was 'entirely subservient to the Macedonian Revolutionary Organisation, which really put them in power', and recent information to the Foreign Office from secret sources showed the intimate connection between the Macedonian Revolutionary Organization and the present Bulgarian Government.[36]

The warning that Bateman had in mind, minuted Sir William Tyrrell, would 'be a little premature at present', but the Foreign Office should keep it up its sleeve for possible future use.[37]

On the next day, 30 October, the Council convened for its last meeting during this special session. The work of evacuation and the re-occupation by the Bulgars and the Greeks of their own frontier posts was verified by the military attachés.[38] The Council's immediate task of bringing an end to the hostilities was completed.

[36] Minute by C. Howard Smith, 29 Oct. 1925. File 13309, FO/371/10672, PRO.

[37] Minute by Sir W.T., 29 Oct. 1925. File 13309, FO/371/10672, PRO.

[38] League of Nations, *Official Journal*, 6th year, 1925, pp. 1713–17.

In the French Foreign Ministry, Jules Laroche, Director of Political Affairs, expressed great satisfaction with the League's settlement of the incident. The world organization, he informed the American Ambassador, Myron T. Herrick, 'had really done valuable service', since the frontier incident was more serious than realized. Information from Istanbul had indicated that Turkey was prepared to profit by trouble in the Balkans. Indeed the Turks, according to Laroche, were 'believed to have informed the Bulgarians that if they wished to carry the matter further, they could count on the support of Turkey'.[39] Chamberlain was no less pleased; he wrote that the world organization had 'secured a great and legitimate success' in this affair. 'The Greeks behaved very badly', he added, 'but were quickly brought to book by the League and that alone prevented war'.[40] In London, reading the minutes of the last meeting of the League Council and those that had preceded it, Bateman minuted that there had been 'some plain speaking here and the whole question [had been] put in a nutshell'.[41] And so it had.

The Commission of Inquiry: Greece Must Pay

Writing to Rumbold, the President of the Commission of Inquiry, on 31 October, Lampson apologized for the inconvenience to which he was being subjected. He explained that it was Chamberlain's own idea that the president of the Commission 'should be a diplomat of high rank', and when this was placed before the League Council, it had welcomed the suggestion and expressed the desire that the president should be a member of the British diplomatic service. The Greek-Bulgarian incident, Lampson continued, had so far been a great success for the world organization and the Council was especially anxious that it should be carried through to a successful finish. If this could be done, it would be 'a good step forward in enhancing the prestige of the League and be an effective warning to the Balkans not to embark in future on offensive operations so light-heartedly'. He noted that he had asked the League Secretariat to send all the pertinent papers to Rumbold in Madrid, and he

[39] Herrick (Paris) to the Sec. of State, no. 5670, 2 Nov. 1925. File 768.74/236, Record Group 59, NA.
[40] Austen Chamberlain to Ida Chamberlain, 31 Oct. 1925. Chamberlain Papers.
[41] Minute by C.H.B. attached to the Council's minutes of 26, 27, 28, 29, and 30 Oct. 1925. File 13309, FO/371/10672, PRO.

expected that Rumbold by this point would himself be in contact with the Secretariat. Needless to say, all the necessary arrangements would be handled by the League Secretariat.

There was one point, Lampson observed, in the Council's resolution, to which the Foreign Office would like to draw his particular attention. It was proposed that the Commission of Inquiry should attempt to establish the facts which would allow the League Council to fix responsibility for the incident; but the Council also desired to receive from the Commission its recommendations as to what measures could be taken to prevent the repetition of such an incident in the future. To this aspect of the question Chamberlain attached the greatest importance.

Two proposals had been rather vaguely advanced: one, the creation of a demilitarized zone to separate the frontier posts of both states—Bateman's idea; two, the establishment of permanent conciliation boards on the lines envisaged in the Locarno agreements, and found in the Franco-German and Belgian-German Treaties of Arbitration initialled on 16 October, copies of which Lampson enclosed.

The Foreign Office, Lampson explained, would be very pleased if Rumbold 'would give this aspect of the question special attention'. Any recommendation stemming from the Commission following its 'investigation on the spot, would carry great weight and it might enable the Council to induce the parties to accept some practical arrangements for avoiding the recurrence of these frontier incidents'. Perhaps it might be possible to combine both these remedies. The importance of a demilitarized zone could be inferred from the fact that, when the incident erupted, the frontier posts in question were apparently only thirty yards apart.

The Foreign Office did not wish in any way to limit the area of the Commission of Inquiry's suggestions and Lampson only wished to let Rumbold know that London attached quite as much importance to establishing permanent measures for the future prevention of incidents, as to establishing the responsibility for what had occurred. There was no wish to fetter Rumbold's discretion as to what particular means were most suitable to attain the desired end.[42]

Some days later when the Greek Minister, Caclamanos, called at the Foreign Office to discuss the events that had occurred, he was informed by Chamberlain that the Commission's report would have

[42] Lampson to Rumbold, 31 Oct. 1925. File 13309, FO/371/10673, PRO.

to be awaited, as well as any recommendation which the Council might desire to make, based on the Commission's report. Both Greece and Bulgaria had invited the League Council, not only to give a judgement on the frontier incident, but also to proffer suggestions for the future prevention of similar episodes, which might be dangerous to the peace of the Greco-Bulgar frontier. The British Foreign Secretary could in no way forecast what suggestions either the Commission or the Council itself might make. Caclamanos's reference to arbitration and demilitarization caused Chamberlain to note that these suggestions were obvious, since there were examples of them elsewhere. Whether they were suitable instruments for pacifying the Greek frontier, Chamberlain did not know. He felt that, in order to make a decision, more detailed knowledge than he possessed of the physical conditions of the frontier area, and of the other factors in question, would be necessary. As to the creation of a demilitarized zone, it was Caclamanos's opinion that this was impossible because of the existence of komitadji bands in the area.

When Caclamanos attempted to offer some defence and explanation of Greece's action against Bulgaria, Chamberlain observed that, since the case was *sub judice*, he could make no comments on the facts. He did note, however, as he had to Carapanos during the Council's discussions in Paris, that it appeared to him that the measures adopted by Greece were far in excess of the offence committed. He observed that this view was also shared by those who had attended the Council's meetings in Paris. He added that whatever were the merits of the case and assuming that the Bulgarian Government was entirely at fault—and all right was on the side of the Greek Government—he 'could not help feeling the unwisdom of the course taken' by the government in Athens. Greece's relations with Yugoslavia were unsettled and had caused Athens some anxiety. Relations between Greece and Bulgaria had never been good. Turkey's attitude towards Greece was less than reassuring. Under these conditions, a policy of great prudence was necessary and this was all the more desirable since Greece was in need of economic credits, and an incident like that which had occurred was sure to alarm investors and make it impossible for Athens to raise money. To these sound comments Caclamanos appears to have made no response.[43]

[43] Chamberlain to Cheetham, 4 Nov. 1925. File 13309, File FO/371/10673, PRO; Chamberlain Papers.

Several days after this interview, the Commission of Inquiry convened for the first time. It was decided at this sitting of the Commission that on their way to the Greek-Bulgarian frontier they should stop at Belgrade for forty-eight hours in order to interview Ninčić, the Yugoslav Foreign Minister. It was felt it would be useful to ascertain Ninčić's views on the recent incident, as well as those of the Yugoslav Government.

When the Commission was received by Ninčić on 9 November, he explained that he had never assumed a grave view of the recent incident. He believed that it would somehow be settled without any serious consequences. His government had during the course of the incident adopted an attitude of absolute impartiality on the question. When asked by Rumbold whether the League's intervention had made an impression in the Balkans, Ninčić reversed his position and admitted that if the incident had been allowed to develop, a serious situation might have arisen, and paid tribute to the League's quick action.

Ninčić's own view was that a demilitarized zone between Greece and Bulgaria would prove to be impracticable. It would be a no-man's-land and an area for actions by komitadjis and brigands. It became obvious to the Commission that Ninčić was preoccupied with the report that it intended to advocate a demilitarized zone, possibly anticipating that such a zone might then have to be extended to the Yugoslav-Bulgar and Yugoslav-Greek frontiers. To Ninčić's remarks the Commission made no reply.

Actually Ninčić's anxieties were premature, for the Commission had already decided that a demilitarized zone along the Greek-Bulgar frontier would be impracticable because of the mountainous terrain there, and because the railway connecting Greek Macedonia and Western Thrace ran at a distance of only a few kilometres from the Bulgarian frontier. The Commission thought it wise, however, to maintain the impression that it was interested in a demilitarized zone in order that the Greek Government might accept, in principle, suggestions of a less radical nature.

The possibility of a demilitarized zone drove Ninčić to talk at some length about the komitadji danger. The Yugoslav Government, he maintained, was not in any way afraid of these raiders. In fact, their activities lately had decreased; he described the measures taken by the Yugoslav Government along the Bulgarian frontier to curb komitadji activities. Ninčić thought that the members of the

Macedonian Revolutionary Organization were carrying on some sort of internecine warfare in Bulgaria. Indeed, they were now killing more Bulgars than Yugolsavs or Greeks. He thought that the komitadji question had actually ceased to be an external threat to his country, though it continued to be an internal threat to the Bulgarian Government.

When the Commission arrived at the frontier, where they stayed for three days, a number of Greek deputations appealed to them. Their complaints in every case were of komitadji incursions and actions. On the whole, however, these deputations did not impress the Commission and they proved an embarrassment to the official from the Greek Foreign Ministry who was attached to the Commission during its stay in Greece. Indeed, the official regretted that the deputations had presented themselves to the Commission, 'since they were doing no good to the Greek cause'.

Because it was impossible for the Commission as a whole to investigate all the districts in Bulgarian territory invaded by the Greeks, it divided itself into three subcommittees. A complete examination was then made of Petrich and of the ten invaded villages. Material damage to houses in the invaded region appeared to be light. On the other hand, stocks of cereals, tobacco, and cotton had been removed by the invading Greeks. Similarly cattle had been driven away, either by the invading Greek military or by Greek villagers living near the frontier who had followed the troops into Bulgarian territory.

On the Commission's arrival in Athens, it was subjected, as one would have expected, to an account of the komitadji danger. However, even General Pangalos had to admit that no komitadji incursion had occurred for about eighteen months. Alluding to the invasion of Bulgaria, Pangalos explained that his orders had been the result of alarming reports dispatched by the Greek military at the frontier. He believed that under the same circumstances any other government would have acted in the same way. He maintained that Athens had welcomed the League's intervention and would do all it could to help strengthen its power. Pangalos then added, however, that Athens did not always have reason to be satisfied with the League's attitude towards Greece, an obvious allusion to the Corfu Incident of several years before, and one which did not escape General Ferrario, the Italian representative on the Commission. General Ferrario subsequently suggested that, if Rumbold thought it fit, he should inform Pangalos that the Corfu Incident was in no way analogous with the Greek invasion of Bulgarian territory. Rumbold, however, did not adopt his Italian colleague's suggestion.

In his own talk with Pangalos, Rumbold told the Greek dictator 'quite frankly' that Greece had complicated matters for the League by violating Article 10 of the Covenant, which he then read to him. Pangalos, Rumbold noted, 'had probably never heard' of Article 10 of the League Covenant. When Pangalos heard the article read to him, he and Kanakaris Roufos, who had replaced Hadjikyriakos as Foreign Minister, both agreed that the 'Greeks had in fact violated the article in question'.

After examining at the border various Greek officers involved in the incident and the subsequent advance into Bulgaria, General Serrigny, the French representative on the Commission, and General Ferrario had come to certain conclusions as to the military steps which might be taken to avoid the repetition of similar incidents. While the Chief of the Greek General Staff was receptive and ready to accept the suggestions in principle, the reaction in Sofia was less favourable. Nevertheless the Bulgars allowed the Commission to suppose that Sofia might accept certain of their suggestions. It was evident to the Commission that Sofia pretended to fear that, if they accepted the services of a neutral officer—as suggested by the Commission—in connection with the modification of frontier supervision, an officer who could also serve on the conciliation commission proposed by the Commission, this might lead to the establishment of one more international commission. This pretended Bulgarian fear, which the Commission felt was anyway unjustified, appeared to the Commission to have been put forward as an excuse for rejecting that particular suggestion. Kalfoff and Minkoff held the view that, while it would be useful to have the conciliation commission proposed by the Rumbold Commission in the background, the Bulgarian Government would want to settle frontier incidents with the Greeks as far as possible by direct talks between Sofia and Athens.

During its stay in Sofia the Commission also had an audience with King Boris, who alluded a number of times and very emphatically to the satisfaction given to his country by the swift and energetic action of the League Council. The king characterized the League's intervention as a turning-point in Balkan history. It was

Rumbold's impression that, because of the League's action, the Bulgarian Government now felt that it had a friend and that it had emerged from its period of post-war isolation.

On his way back to Geneva, Rumbold had another interview with Ninčić in Belgrade on 27 November. Asked by Ninčić about the Commission's experiences, Rumbold gave no indication of the contents of the Commission's report. He restricted himself to replying that the Commission's recommendations would be suited to the geographical features of the Greek-Bulgarian frontier and to existing Greek-Bulgarian arrangements. Ninčić was still anxious about a demilitarized zone and brought up the question again, alluding to the suggestion 'as not being a question of practical politics'.[44]

The Greeks would be found guilty in the Commission's report, the American chargé d'affaires in Sofia, Cable, informed the Department of State. They would have to pay damages and the Greeks had 'expressed a willingness to do so'. It had also been determined that the komitadjis were in no way responsible for the incident. It was Rumbold's desire, according to Cable, to hit upon a solution that would place the Greeks in a more favourable position. Rumbold feared that the possible repercussions of the Commission's report in Greece might overthrow the Pangalos government and lead to the accusation that the League of Nations had been responsible for the dictator's fall.[45]

The sensitive internal Greek situation was a factor that could not be disregarded. In Geneva, on the night of 1 December, the Greek chargé d'affaires in Bern, Vassili Dendramis, called on the French Director of the League's Political Section, Paul Mantoux, to discuss the Commission of Inquiry's coming report. Mantoux accordingly summoned a British member of the League Secretariat, Major G. H. F. Abraham, also of the Political Section, who had been attached to the Commission. At the outset of this three-man discussion, Dendramis explained that, though he had no instructions and no knowledge of what was in the Rumbold report, he believed that, should it call for Greek payment to Bulgaria, such payment might generate 'serious difficulties in the internal situation

---

[44] Rumbold (Geneva) to Chamberlain, 1 Dec. 1925. File 13309, FO/371/10673, PRO.
[45] Cable (Sofia) to the Dept. of State, 23 Nov. 1925. File 768.74/238, Record Group 59, NA.

in Greece'. Greek public opinion would not easily accept the 'humiliation' of an indemnity to Bulgaria. He therefore suggested that the Commission of Inquiry 'might consider the possibility of recommending' that Bulgaria be authorized to reduce the reparations owed to Greece under the Treaty of Neuilly by any sum that might otherwise be awarded to it by the Rumbold Commission.

Major Abraham replied that this proposal appeared to be a question entirely outside the Commission's competence and probably outside the League's. He pointed out that there were two types of indemnity provided for by the Council in its resolution. The first was for local material damage—and the Commission's decision on this was final—and the second was of a more general order, on which the Commission was obliged to make recommendations to the Council. As to the first, Abraham noted, although the payment was to be from one government to another, the sum given was intended to be handed over immediately to the persons who had suffered losses as a result of the Greek invasion. He pointed out that this group were mostly peasants. Dendramis queried whether there was a time limit imposed for the payment of this sum. Abraham answered in the negative. The gist of this interview was quickly reported by Abraham to Rumbold.

Abraham, in writing to the League's Secretary-General, Sir Eric Drummond, suggested that since Dendramis might raise this question again, it was worth keeping in mind that Greece, both in the League, before the Rumbold Commission, and in the press was constantly urging that treaties of compulsory arbitration were essential between itself and its surrounding neighbours, and had often expressed the desire that the world organization assist in every possible way. Greece had accepted the Council's arbitration on the subject of indemnities with regard to the present incident. Indeed, Abraham pointed out that Greece itself had presented a bill for £142,000. He thought it would be a bad precedent for the principle Greece was advocating if Athens made difficulties about paying an indemnity under the first arbitration it had accepted under the League's auspices. If he were not mistaken, Bulgarian reparation payments were about £90,000 a year, of which Greece was entitled to from 10 to 20 per cent. It would therefore take from two and a half to five years to liquidate the indemnity established by the Commission, which was thirty million Bulgarian leva (about £45,000 in 1925). The entire action of the League in this question, he concluded, 'would also be depreciated' by the proposed Greek plan.[46]

On the following day, it became clearer that Dendramis's probe in Geneva was no personal move but rather part of a concerted drive by the Greeks. In Athens, Cheetham was handed a long note from Roufos, the Greek Foreign Minister. The note was a condemnation of the Rumbold Commission's report, a copy of which had been communicated to the Greek Government. Roufos felt that the report's conclusions were neither just nor impartial. He hoped that the League Council would not agree with the report and that the British delegate to the Council would receive instructions to this effect. In the note's penultimate paragraph was expressed the desire that any indemnity to be paid by Greece to Bulgaria should instead be deducted from the war reparations owed to Greece by Bulgaria[47]—the point that Dendramis had made in Geneva, in his conversation with Mantoux and Major Abraham of the League Secretariat.

In his covering note to Chamberlain, Cheetham explained that on the previous day, 1 December—the same day Dendramis called on Mantoux and Major Abraham—he had been asked to call on Roufos. The new Greek Foreign Minister had spoken to him to the same purpose as the enclosed note. Roufos had prefaced his remarks by informing Cheetham confidentially that the Cabinet had experienced 'some difficulty' in inducing Pangalos 'to behave in a reasonable manner' when the Commission's findings were communicated to him confidentially. The British Minister thought it quite conceivable, he observed to the Foreign Secretary, that Pangalos had never read the text of the League Covenant himself, and that accordingly 'he was in reality unaware of its exact contents'.

The point that Roufos was most concerned about, according to Cheetham, was the payment of an indemnity to the Bulgars. The Greek Foreign Minister during their talk had 'pressed with some vigour' the suggestion that any sums to be paid by Greece to Bulgaria as the result of the Commission's findings should be deducted from the war reparation payments due to Greece from Bulgaria. Roufos had also stated very frankly that under the present

---

[46] Abraham to the Secretary-General through Mantoux, 2 Dec. 1925. File 13309, FO/371/10673, PRO.

[47] Roufos to Cheetham, no. 17263, 2 Dec. 1925. French Text. File 13309, FO/371/10673, PRO.

financial conditions his government would be in no position to pay an indemnity to Bulgaria in cash. Cheetham tended to believe this, for he pointed out to Chamberlain that during the last six weeks it had become apparent that the Athens government had no cash at its disposal beyond such amounts as were required for current administrative expenses and supplies of immediate necessity. Payments in all fields had been deferred and fiscal obligations disregarded. It was, for example, useless to try to call attention to Britain's commercial claims or to demand satisfaction for British owners of properties which had been requisitioned. Cheetham presumed, however, that the Athens government could still find means in one way or another to comply with its obligations.[48]

On the following day, 3 December, the Greek case was again presented to the British Foreign Office, this time by Caclamanos, who called on Lampson at the Central Department. He arrived bearing a telegram which he had just received from Athens and which he was instructed to present to the Foreign Office. Caclamanos explained that Athens had received from the Rumbold Commission a copy of the report which the Commission would send to the League Council, and her government was disturbed to discover that this report placed much of the blame on Greece for the recent border incident.

At this point Lampson thought it desirable to interrupt Caclamanos, pointing out that the Foreign Office had received no copy of the Rumbold Commission's report and consequently he was in ignorance of its contents. Moreover, as the matter was *sub judice* and would be presented to the Foreign Secretary, Chamberlain, as a member of the League Council at its forthcoming session, it would obviously be improper if he, Lampson, were to express any opinion or make any comment upon anything that Caclamanos might say with regard to the contents of the report itself. If this were understood, Lampson was willing to hear what Caclamanos had to say.

The Greek Minister stated that he fully understood the attitude that Lampson had expressed, which was exactly what he had anticipated, and on this understanding he would proceed to make the representations imposed upon him by his government. Athens noted that no compensation would be given to Greece for the death

[48] Cheetham (Athens) to Chamberlain, no. 390, 2 Dec. 1925. File 13309, FO/371/10673, PRO.

of the Greek officer who had attempted to stop the fighting and had been shot while carrying a white flag. As to the indemnity that would have to be given to Bulgaria by Greece, his government felt that ten million Bulgarian leva for moral damage and twenty million Bulgarian leva for material damage, thirty million Bulgarian leva in all, was too drastic. He was instructed by Athens to appeal to Sir Austen Chamberlain's 'sense of justice' and to beg that the League Council should not give 'too sharp a character of unilateral punition to Greece'. Caclamanos then observed that if the Council did, in fact, award damages against his country, the latter would not, of course, expect that cash payment to Bulgaria would be called for, but rather that the Athens government would be allowed to reduce the sum of war reparation payments due from Bulgaria to Greece.

Lampson replied that he would take note of Caclamanos's communication, but that, as he had made clear from the beginning of the interview, he did not propose to make any special comment upon what Caclamanos had said beyond the obvious one that the decision was with the League Council, which would doubtless consider every view placed before it.

Before departing, Caclamanos dropped his official role as the Greek Minister accredited to the Court of St. James. He gave Lampson to understand that he, Caclamanos, 'personally had no doubt of the foolishness of the action of his government in invading Bulgaria as they had done'. Caclamanos pleaded with Lampson that the present Pangalos dictatorship 'was composed largely of military men who had no knowledge of statesmanship, and he begged that Greece as a country should not be made to suffer too severely through the ignorance of her present leaders'.[49] To this comment Lampson appears to have made no reply.

In Geneva, however, the Greek drive had found no supporters in the League Secretariat. Paul Mantoux, the French Director of the League's Political Section, was especially unreceptive. Writing to the Secretary-General, Drummond, on the same day, 3 December, Mantoux expressed the opinion that the Council should describe in very clear terms in its final resolution exactly how the recommendations of the Rumbold Commission concerning the indemnity should be executed. This would remove the possibility

[49] Memorandum of Conversation with the Greek Minister by Mr. Lampson, 3 Dec. 1925. File 13309, FO/371/10673, PRO.

of delay if the matter were left to the Greeks and Bulgars, and would lead to immediate compensation for the victims of the incident. Delay in payment of the indemnity would greatly detract from the value and effect of the League Council's prompt and decisive action. Mantoux was also ready to reply to the Greek argument that there was no material difference between the damages of the war and the damages caused by the recent incident— an argument to justify the deduction of Greece's payment to Bulgaria from the reparations owed by Bulgaria to Greece—and that, correspondingly, there was no reason to give immediate priority to the victims of the incident. To Mantoux it appeared impossible that the Council would admit such a resemblance between the consequences of the war and the consequences arising from hostilities engaged in during a time of peace, by a member of the world organization, contrary to the stipulations of the League Covenant.[50]

The Secretary-General agreed that it was desirable to separate the question of the indemnity due by Greece to Bulgaria from the question of reparation payments due to Greece from Bulgaria. It was Drummond's opinion that the League Council should establish a definite time limit for the payment to be made by the Greeks, say, perhaps two and a half months, so that a report could be given on the subject at the Council's March meeting. On the other hand, if the Greeks and Bulgars decided of their own accord to come to an agreement as to the method of payment, the League Council could make no objection to this agreement, provided that Sofia was completely satisfied in the matter and had accepted the arrangement freely. He believed that all these Secretariat minutes should be shown privately to the Council *rapporteur*[51]—Sir Austen Chamberlain.

The Greek drive was giving cause for uneasiness in Geneva. That same day, Sir Alexander Cadogan, a First Secretary of the Foreign Office and an assistant to the British delegation to the League of Nations, informed the Foreign Office that the Secretary-General, Drummond, had told him that Greek circles in the League of Nations were most uneasy as to the attitude which the Greek

[50] Mantoux to Drummond, 3 Dec. 1925. French Text. File 13309, FO/371/10673, PRO.
[51] Note by the Secretary-General, Sir E.D., 3 Dec. 1925. File 13309, FO/371/10673, PRO.

delegation might adopt at the coming Council meeting, in view of the Rumbold Commission's report. The fear was that the Greeks might even refuse to attend the Council meeting at all. Cadogan asked the Foreign Office whether it would consider the possibility of instructing Cheetham to urge on the Athens government the necessity of accepting the League Council's award.[52]

In forwarding this news from Cadogan to Cheetham, Chamberlain pointed out that the Greek refusal to accept the Council's findings would place the Athens government 'still further in the wrong and prolong [a] dispute which all wish now to see terminated'. He did not believe that Athens could contemplate breaking the pledge that it had given the Council or had any intention of acting as had been suggested in Geneva. However, if Cheetham found that Geneva's apprehensions were well founded, he should inform the Pangalos government immediately that Chamberlain had 'received this information with great surprise' and was hardly able to give it credit. He was also to point out that Greece's breach of its pledge to accept the Council's decision 'might have very serious consequences for Greece and would make friends of Greece despair of her future'. Cheetham was to urge the Greek Government to 'pursue [the] only course consistent with Greek dignity and with their obligations as members of the League of Nations'. Chamberlain, however, wished Cheetham to be sure that there was ground for such an intervention, before he took any action.[53]

Cheetham's response soon followed. His own information, he told the Foreign Office, gave no reason to suspect the attitude of Greece's delegation at Geneva. If Rentis, who had been chosen to head the delegation at Geneva, had authority to act in the manner suggested by Sir Eric Drummond, he had concealed his instructions from Cheetham. Rentis had called on Cheetham prior to his departure for Geneva, and during that interview had given no hint of the development that was apprehended. The only information that Cheetham had received was Roufos's note of 2 December, which he had already forwarded to the Foreign Office. The Greek Foreign Minister's main preoccupation, Cheetham opined, was that any indemnity to be paid by Greece to Bulgaria should be deducted from the war reparations owed by Bulgaria to Greece.

[52] F.O. to Athens, no. 158, 5 Dec. 1925, repeating Geneva to the F.O., no. 386, 3 Dec. 1925. File 953, FO/286/916, PRO.
[53] F.O. to Athens, no. 159, 5 Dec. 1925. File 953, FO/286/916, PRO.

Roufos's argument was that Greece was unable to furnish the required sum. Indeed, Roufos had previously informed Cheetham that the Greek Government had welcomed Geneva's intervention and counted on the League's future support in Balkan affairs. That same morning Roufos had called on him at the legation. He had during this interview again referred to his prior suggestion about how the indemnity should be paid to the Bulgars. He had also offered to communicate to Cheetham any news that he might receive from Geneva.

Cheetham then added that several days before he had called on General Pangalos about a British telephone concession. The Greek dictator received him in a very friendly manner and had expressed his regrets that Cheetham had recently been unable to accept his invitation to an official dinner. To Cheetham it appeared difficult to reconcile Pangalos's and Roufos's attitude with the suspicion that Greece might not accept the Council's award. He therefore supposed that Roufos's note of 2 December 'was intended to convey a dignified protest without involving any breach' of Greece's obligations to the world organization.[54]

On the day following the dispatch of this message, 7 December, the League Council convened in Geneva to reconsider the Greek-Bulgarian Incident and the report of the Rumbold Commission in particular. The President during this session of the Council was the Italian representative, Vittorio Scialoja. Bulgaria's representative was Kalfoff, the Foreign Minister, who accepted the Commission's report expressing reservations only on the question of the indemnity which he thought was inadequate, and on the hiring of neutral officers who would serve on the conciliation commission proposed by the Commission and already mentioned to the Bulgarian Government by Rumbold, when he had visited Sofia.

Rentis's long reply on behalf of the Greeks was predictable. He thanked the Council for its intervention in the incident, and on behalf of his government accepted the Rumbold Commission's suggested military proposals to be instituted along the Greek-Bulgarian frontier—the neutral officers scheme. He also accepted the Commission's report of the facts as to what had occurred at the frontier when the incident had erupted. On the other hand, he requested reparations from Bulgaria for the loss of life suffered by the Greeks, especially the death of the Greek officer carrying the white

[54] Athens to the F.O., no. 213, 6 Dec. 1925. File 953, FO/286/916, PRO.

flag of truce. Indeed, the Rumbold Commission admitted that Greece had valid claims but felt they should be disallowed. It was for the League Council to decide that question, Rentis noted, not the Commission. In a discussion of the Greek invasion of Bulgaria, Rentis argued that coercion was justified in certain instances, as the Council itself had admitted in March of 1924 when it had accepted the opinion of the Commission of Jurists established to deal with certain legal questions arising from the Corfu Incident of 1923.[55]

The discussion of the question continued at the second meeting of the Council, also in public, later that day. After further statements by Kalfoff and Rentis, Sir Austen Chamberlain, the Council's *rapporteur* on this question, offered a proposal. This was that he should have the assistance of two Council 'colleagues for the consideration of the report' of the Rumbold Commission and the statements made by Kalfoff and Rentis. The consequence which the Council's decision might have for what Chamberlain called the 'jurisprudence of the League of Nations, was so important' that the British Foreign Secretary would be pleased if he could have the assistance of his Council colleagues in preparing a report for the League Council, 'so that the whole responsibility of preparing this report should not rest upon his shoulders'. To this proposal the Council agreed and Paul Hymans of Belgium and Viscount Kikujiro Ishii of Japan were chosen. The Council then decided to postpone discussion of the question until it had received the report which would be presented to it by Chamberlain, Hymans, and Viscount Ishii.[56]

On the following day, 8 December, the Rumbold Commission spent a good part of the day questioning the Bulgarian and Greek representatives separately. These labours led to an agreement to accept in a slightly modified form the military recommendations tendered by the Commission. The agreement was written up and then forwarded to Chamberlain.[57]

---

[55] League of Nations, *Official Journal*, 7th year, 1926, pp. 108–17. The ambiguous opinion accepted by the Council from the Commission of Jurists in March of 1924 was as follows: 'Coercive measures which are not intended to constitute acts of war may or may not be consistent with the provisions of Articles 12 to 15 of the Covenant, and it is for the Council, when the dispute has been submitted to it, to decide immediately, having due regard to all the circumstances of the case and to the nature of the measures adopted, whether it should recommend the maintenance or the withdrawal of such measures.'

[56] League of Nations, *Official Journal*, 7th year, 1926, pp. 117–18.

[57] Lampson to Howard Smith, 12 Dec. 1925. File 13309, FO/371/10673,

On the same day one of the questions being examined by the British was whether the Greek argument that they could not pay any indemnity was valid. Accordingly, Lampson forwarded to Sir Otto Niemeyer, Controller of Finance in the British Treasury, a request from Chamberlain for his views on the Greek suggestion to deduct any indemnity given to Bulgaria against Bulgarian war reparations owing to Greece. The facts that were revealed, Lampson wrote, were: one, the Rumbold Commission was unanimously opposed to Greece being allowed to write off its payments; two, the Foreign Office had heard from Athens and elsewhere that the Greeks would endeavour to insist on that method of payment; three, could the Foreign Office, Lampson asked Niemeyer, 'give *convincing* reasons' why Athens's request could not be met by citing, for example, normal reparations procedure, or unfairness to the Bulgarians; and four, there remained a further possibility, that of saying that the twenty million Bulgarian leva due to the victims had to be an immediate payment, but that the ten million Bulgarian leva could be a book transaction, as it was an affair between governments.

On the surface, Lampson added, it might be better to insist that the Greeks make an immediate cash payment. In closing his note to Niemeyer, he pointed out that Chamberlain had also raised the question of Greece's capacity to pay any indemnity to Bulgaria.[58]

Niemeyer's reply was composed that same day. His attitude was no more friendly to the Greeks than that of Mantoux, Drummond, or Major Abraham. It was Niemeyer's opinion that the Greek suggestion to deduct any indemnity owed to Bulgaria from war reparations owed to Greece by Bulgaria was merely a way of saying that, instead of receiving its indemnity now, Bulgaria would receive its indemnity over a period of about two years. It was obvious that such an arrangement was not what the Rumbold Commission intended. One might also assume that if payment of the indemnity was to be postponed, the total amount would have been increased

---

PRO. See also Réunion de la Commission d'Enquête, sous la Présidence de Sir Horace Rumbold tenue à Genève, Mardi le 8 Décembre 1925, pour l'Audition des Représentants de la Bulgarie et de la Grèce au Conseil. File 13309, FO/371/10673, PRO, and Commentaires de la Commission d'Enquête sur les Discours des Représentants de la Bulgarie et de la Grèce du [8] Décembre au Sujet du Rapport de la Commission d'Enquête sur les Incidents Gréco-Bulgare. File 13309, FO/371/10673, PRO.

[58] Lampson to Niemeyer, 8 Dec. 1925. File 13309, FO/371/10673, PRO.

by the Commission 'to give a present value' of thirty million Bulgarian leva.

Niemeyer correctly pointed out that the Greeks several years before had not postponed their payment to the Italians in order to hasten their evacuation of the island of Corfu which Mussolini had occupied, following the murder of the Italian members of the international commission delimiting the Greek-Albanian border. It was, of course, possible to spread payments, but it was not necessary to make this dependent on the reparation payments. This introduced an unnecessary complication and though for the moment he saw no possibility in doing it—whether it was desirable to involve the League in moral responsibility for reparation payments was, he felt, a political question—only a bold person would prophesy what might develop with regard to war reparations in the future.

If Athens received x-amount of money from war reparations into her treasury, he continued, she could pay that sum from her treasury to Bulgaria 'without a *formal* connection between the two payments'. According to British Treasury figures, several years would have to pass before the reparation payments that Greece would receive from Bulgaria would cover the indemnity to be given to Bulgaria by Greece.

Niemeyer therefore thought the suggestion to link the indemnity payment to reparations was unfair to Bulgaria and involved, at any rate, a risk of future complications. Though it was very difficult to speak with confidence about the Greek budget, the Greeks maintained that it was balanced at about £20 million. It was inconceivable to Niemeyer that in a budget of that size the Greeks could not pay an indemnity of £45,000. Lastly, Niemeyer noted, Greece had always maintained to Great Britain that it had plenty of cash for naval expenditure or for the allocation of revenue to special loans.[59]

While this exchange was going on between Lampson and Niemeyer, Major Abraham of the League Secretariat had put together a rough draft of the report that Chamberlain's subcommittee would present to the League Council. Copies of this rough draft were also given to Lampson and Sir Cecil Hurst of the Foreign Office's Legal Department. On the evening of 10 December, Rumbold, Hurst, and Lampson called on the Foreign Secretary, Chamberlain, at his hotel and as a result of this interview,

[59] Niemeyer to Lampson, 8 Dec. 1925. File 13309, FO/371/10672, PRO.

re-drafted several sections of Abraham's draft report. Major Abraham was summoned that night and he returned to his office with the re-drafted report. By eleven-thirty that night the typed copies of the revised report were once more in the hands of Messrs. Chamberlain, Rumbold, Hurst, and Lampson.[60]

The next day, 11 December, Major Abraham gave Lampson, who forwarded it to Chamberlain, the intra-Secretariat correspondence dealing with the Greek proposal that any indemnity to Bulgaria be written off against Bulgarian war reparation payments to Greece. The Secretary-General, Drummond, wished that Chamberlain be given these papers as the Council's *rapporteur*. The Secretary-General and the Secretariat of the League, Lampson noted, were 'strongly opposed' to the Greek proposal. So was Lampson. The League was in no way involved in how Greece raised the money to pay the indemnity to Bulgaria. If Athens desired to raise the proposal, it would have to contact the Reparations Commission at Paris, within whose province the proposal lay.[61] That day there was a meeting of the Council's subcommittee, chaired by Chamberlain. The revised draft of the report was examined and a few alterations made, 'some mere matters of form, others of fundamental importance'. The Council subcommittee then had a short discussion with the members of the Rumbold Commission. They were then joined by the Bulgarian representative, and after his departure by his Greek counterpart. Both representatives gave their views and then formally confirmed the agreement which they had made with the Rumbold Commission on 8 December. The only important point raised was by Rentis, who challenged the basis on which the Rumbold Commission had assessed the damages—the twenty million Bulgarian leva—which had to be paid to Bulgaria by Greece for the removal of property, stock, crops, etc. Before Chamberlain's subcommittee dispersed, it was arranged that the Rumbold Commission would consider and report to the subcommittee on Rentis's challenge of their figures for the indemnity due to Bulgaria; and that a small drafting committee composed of Major Abraham, Rumbold, and Lampson should meet in the afternoon and examine the revised draft report and alter it wherever necessary.

[60] Lampson to Howard Smith, 12 Dec. 1925. File 13309, FO/371/10673, PRO.
[61] Lampson to Chamberlain, 11 Dec. 1925. File 13309, FO/371/10673, PRO.

Leaving this meeting of the subcommittee Lampson met Thanassis Aghnides, a Greek national and a senior official of the League Secretariat's Political Section. Aghnides had been standing with the Greek delegation when Lampson emerged from the meeting of the subcommittee. He immediately 'button-holed' Lampson and began talking to him in a general manner about the Greek situation. This soon led to the question of the Rumbold Commission's report, at which point Aghnides took what Lampson described as 'an extremely sensible line'. Aghnides explained that he had impressed on Rentis the 'extreme unwisdom of drawing red herrings across the track' of the Rumbold Commission's report. The soundest tack for Greece to adopt was to accept the report's recommendations. It was completely in Athens's interest to cause no trouble. Indeed, if seen in the right light, this question might establish a very valuable precedent which could be invoked by Greece itself in case of future trouble with Yugoslavia. The less difficulty made by Greece now, when it was doubtless in the wrong, the greater would be its 'justification in appealing to the League for similar action' when Greece itself 'was in the future the aggrieved party'.

Lampson replied that this 'was a very wise line to adopt' and he begged Aghnides to continue urging it with Rentis, which Aghnides said he would do. Aghnides then said that there was one matter on which he was very anxious that Lampson should do what he could to make it easier for his country 'to swallow the very humiliating pill' which the League was now going to administer to it. In the Rumbold Commission's report, his country was formally found to be guilty of a breach of the League Covenant. Aghnides did not deny that the finding was perfectly correct. On the other hand, could not the subcommittee's report bring out the fact that Athens 'had not deliberately and of set purpose violated the Covenant'? If this could be done, it would make it much easier for Greek public opinion to accept the Council's decision.

Lampson responded that in 'no court of law could it be pleaded that ignorance of the law was an adequate excuse of its violation'. At the same time the League was an instrument for conciliation and there was certainly no desire to make the Greek position needlessly difficult. He would, therefore, bear Aghnides's point in mind and see how far the subcommittee could write something into the report to meet it. The result of this suggestion by Aghnides was that the subcommittee incorporated into its report a section in which it alluded specifically to the fact that the Athens government had undoubtedly been led astray by messages distorted in the transmission. However, it felt bound to add—the particular passage was drafted by General Serrigny—that had the information received by Athens been completely correct, the military measures adopted by the Greeks were even so strategically unjustified.

Later that day the small drafting committee established by Chamberlain's subcommittee convened. In addition to Major Abraham, Rumbold, and Lampson, they were joined by three other members of the Rumbold Commission, one of whom was the French representative, General Serrigny. The latter was of great assistance and with his help the drafting committee soon went through the report and drafted the additional paragraphs needed to execute the directions they had received from Chamberlain's subcommittee earlier that day. The draft report was thus revised a second time and was ready for perusal before dinner. Late that night it was examined by Chamberlain, copies having been also dispatched to Hymans and Viscount Ishii. The arrangement was that the following morning, 12 December, Chamberlain would ascertain from his two Council colleagues what modifications they might wish to suggest, in addition to those which Chamberlain himself had made, most of which were mainly matters of phraseology. If the report was acceptable to all three members of the subcommittee, copies would then be given to the Greeks and Bulgars so that they would both have time to consider the terms of the report before it was presented to the Council for final adoption.[62]

When presented with the report of the subcommittee on 12 December, the Bulgarian representative accepted it without qualifications. Rentis, on the other hand, asked for an interview with the Foreign Secretary, Chamberlain, to advance certain arguments. Accordingly a meeting was arranged for 6 p.m. at which Major Abraham and Lampson were also present. Rentis began the conversation by stating that he completely understood the principle on which the subcommittee's report was based. It was in the interests of the world that this principle be adopted, for his own country as

<hr>

[62] Lampson to Howard Smith, 12 Dec. 1925. File 13309, FO/371/10673, PRO. See also Différend Gréco-Bulgare: Réunion du Comité du Conseil sous la Présidence de Sir Austen Chamberlain séance du 11 décembre 1925 à 10 heures. File 13309, FO/371/10673, PRO.

much as for others. At the same time he presumed that no one desired to humiliate his country. He asked if something could not be done to make the subcommittee's report more readily acceptable to Greek public opinion? Was it not possible to admit that reparations were also due to Greece?

Chamberlain replied that the subcommittee had carefully examined this question. They had brought it up both with the Rumbold Commission and at the meeting of the subcommittee the previous day and also with Rentis when he had appeared before the subcommittee. It was, however, impossible for the subcommittee to admit that any reparation was due to Greece in view of the circumstances established by the Rumbold Commission for the casualties that had occurred in Bulgarian territory.

Changing his tack, Rentis inquired whether, in that case, reparation could not be made for the casualties suffered before the Greek Army actually invaded Bulgaria. Chamberlain responded that Rentis's query raised a question of principle which he would not admit. He would be pleased to modify phrases or expressions in the report which Rentis desired to see altered. But he could not agree to the modification of a fundamental principle which had already been accepted by his two colleagues on the subcommittee. At this point Chamberlain referred to the conversation between Lampson and Aghnides and the latter's comment that what would be especially difficult for Greek public opinion to accept was the Rumbold Commission's categorical statement that Greece had violated the League Covenant. Aghnides's suggestion, Chamberlain observed, was that something might be included in the subcommittee's report showing that although there had been a technical violation of the League Covenant, it had been committed only 'because of the ignorance of the provisions of that instrument'. The British Foreign Secretary admitted that he had carefully considered Aghnides's suggestion. He had come to the conclusion, however, that if this were to be included in the report, it would really be a direct censure of General Pangalos, rather than an excuse for Greece's action. Rentis had to remember that ignorance of the law could never be admitted as an excuse for its violation. The Athens government could not plead ignorance of treaties to which they had acceded.

When Rentis again pressed this point, Chamberlain replied that the subcommittee had examined it, and had come to the firm conclusion that they could not allow it. It was true that in its report the subcommittee could have given the actual figures for the compensation allowed for the Greek officer killed when carrying the flag of truce. They had, however, decided against this. The facts were that the Rumbold Commission had itself made allowances for the reparation due to Greece from the death of the Greek officer, and had deducted this amount from the Bulgarian claim. His subcommittee, Chamberlain explained, had satisfied itself that this had been done, and it could not now agree to show how the total amount decided on by the Rumbold Commission was reached. Furthermore, Rentis had to remember that both Athens and Sofia had asked the League Council to settle the incident, and had promised in advance to abide by the Council's decision. The British Foreign Secretary pointed out that what was now a decision against Greece might in the future be invoked by Greece in its own defence, if it was ever the victim in a similar incident.

Chamberlain also made a general observation. In this matter he was in the public eye of his own country. He would be unwilling to sign the subcommittee's report unless he was himself satisfied that he was justified in doing so. He then referred to an obscure allusion made by Rentis in his Council speech of 7 December. According to the British Foreign Secretary, Rentis had said that if Great Britain were to take some immediate action under the terms of the Locarno Treaty before a Council decision could be reached, the British Government would obviously do so at its own risk. He pointed out, however, that everyone at Locarno had agreed that, should one of the signatories take immediate action under the articles of the Locarno Treaty permitting such action, the matter had to come before the League Council, and that the country involved would submit to the Council's decision, even if it had already taken action.

Shifting his ground, Rentis inquired whether, if his country had not actually invaded Bulgaria, the League Council would not have made allowances for the expenses which it had incurred by the transfer of Greek military forces to the frontier, etc. Chamberlain replied that if Rentis desired to press the point further, he could call for Sir Horace Rumbold who would explain more fully the reasons governing the Commission's decision. The facts were, however, quite clear. The Rumbold Commission had found that the Greek officer had been killed. At the same time, they were careful to show that there was no certainty as to who had killed him.

Yet despite this doubt the Commission had considered that the death of an officer under the white flag of truce was a very grave matter, and the Rumbold Commission had explained to Chamberlain and his colleagues on the Council's subcommittee its reason for the scale at which the reparation had been set. The Rumbold Commission's report, however, clearly pointed out that there was, in fact, no proof as to where the bullet that had killed the Greek officer had come from.

Rentis's comment was that it was always his government's intention to seek good relations with the Bulgars, and that the slain Greek officer had ordered his men to cease firing before advancing towards the Bulgarian frontier posts. This impelled Chamberlain to produce the Rumbold Commission's report and read out loud the pertinent passages, showing that no conclusion was possible as to who was responsible for the shot that had killed the Greek officer. The only undisputed fact was that the officer had been killed.

Rentis's point, that no essential alteration in the subcommittee's report was necessary if reparation were awarded to Greece against Bulgaria for the deaths that had occurred before the Greek advance into Bulgaria, moved Chamberlain to state that what Rentis was asking for 'was in fact a very essential alteration'. Chamberlain added that he was ready to do what he could to meet the Greek representative's wishes, but there were certain things he was powerless to do. He had already submitted his report to Hymans and Viscount Ishii. Both had accepted it. He was still in a position to make changes in phraseology. Changes of substance were another matter. Indeed, the Rumbold Commission had in fact studied the very point that Rentis had raised: allowance to the Greeks for expenses incurred in moving troops to the frontier—but it had been rejected. Rentis was reminded that the Rumbold Commission's report had stated that a Greek airplane had flown over Bulgar territory and had not been able to locate any serious Bulgarian troop movements. Similarly, the Greeks themselves had admitted that they thought the incident was a komitadji affair.

Undoubtedly frustrated, Rentis made a veiled allusion to the Corfu Incident of 1923 and 'the apparent differentiation now being made against Greece'. Chamberlain was quick to react. He 'would strongly advise' Rentis, the British Foreign Secretary remarked, 'in his own interests not to insist on this point'. It was very possible that in the years to come, with the development of the League's jurisprudence, the world organization 'would itself say that there was less excuse for measures of coercion'.

Rentis's observation was that he would like to accept the subcommittee's report without any comment. Chamberlain, doubtless irritated, retorted that 'obviously he could not buy M. Rentis's silence'. If Rentis decided to say that he believed the subcommittee's report unjust, well, let him say it. Chamberlain did not think that such a course of action would do Greece any good, but that was for Rentis to decide. The British Foreign Secretary noted that if Rentis had desired to make the objections which he was now making, he might have done so before the subcommittee the previous day. The Greek's rejoinder was that he had not known at that time exactly what Chamberlain's subcommittee would decide to say.

Chamberlain's reaction was to point out that if Rentis meant to imply that he did not accept the subcommittee's report, it was easy to call another meeting of the subcommittee, before which Rentis could appear and reproduce his arguments. However, Chamberlain emphasized the fact that it was impossible to change the report without consulting his colleagues, Hymans and Viscount Ishii. He repeated that Rentis's proposed alteration entailed a fundamental change in the report.

Rentis finally succumbed, remarking that if Sir Austen considered it a fundamental change, he, Rentis, would understand that the subcommittee could not make it. Chamberlain observed that even if the change Rentis desired were made, Bulgaria would then be justified in charging his subcommittee with making a fundamental change in the report. The Greek representative thought that the report as it now stood would not encourage friendly relations between Athens and Sofia and alluded to a statement by Briand in Paris regarding the undesirability of a two-camp division—victors and vanquished.

The British Foreign Secretary replied that what Athens could not accept from an armed Sofia, it could accept with dignity from the League Council. That in itself was one of the League's great points. It was a third party whose proposals could be accepted. He pointed out that the subcommittee's report accepted the view that Greece had acted 'in good faith' and on the basis of 'exaggerated reports from the front'. Moreover, he had been anxious not to insist in the report on such facts as the information supplied by the

Greek airplane which had flown over Bulgarian territory and had spotted no troop movements. That information, he continued, would have reflected upon Pangalos's action, which Rentis would hardly desire. His subcommittee, Chamberlain insisted, had really attempted to make its 'findings as easy as possible for Greece'. Rentis admitted that this was so. With this comment the interview turned to other matters.[63]

Two days later, on the morning of 14 December, the Council took up the question for the last time. The Rumbold Commission, Chamberlain insisted, had contrary to Rentis's criticisms acted correctly. As to the indemnity of thirty million Bulgarian leva awarded to Bulgaria, Greece would have to pay this sum within two months and the Council be informed of the payment. Rentis accepted the report of Chamberlain's subcommittee and thanked the British Foreign Secretary for recognizing in the report that his country 'had acted without premeditation'.[64] Later that morning Rentis informed Lampson how much he appreciated Chamberlain's statement in the Council regarding the part that he, Rentis, had played in settling the question. He was especially appreciative of the passage in the subcommittee's report recognizing that Athens had not acted with premeditation. Rentis reiterated to Lampson the bad reception which the Council's decision was bound to have in Greece. One could only hope, he told Lampson, that as Greek opinion came to recognize the importance of the precedent that the Council had now established and to appreciate its future implications for Greece, public resentment against the decision might subside.

They parted the best of friends. It was Lampson's own feeling that Rentis had conducted himself at the Council session 'both with dignity and great ability in circumstances of the greatest difficulty'. Lampson told Rentis it would have been an unpleasant assignment for any member of the present Greek administration responsible for the border incident to come to the League and plead a lost cause. Therefore it had been very generous of Rentis, who had departed from the Foreign Ministry before the incident erupted, and had therefore no responsibility for it, to come to Geneva to rescue the Athens government in its present difficulties and to take

[63] Record of Conversation between Sir Austen Chamberlain and M. Rentis by M. W. Lampson, 12 Dec. 1925. File 13309, FO/371/10673, PRO.
[64] League of Nations, *Official Journal*, 7th year, 1926, pp. 172–7.

on himself the very disagreeable task of pleading Athens's case before the League. Moreover, everyone at the Council meeting that morning had been struck by the very discreet way in which Rentis had alluded to the new precedent established by the Council. Lampson, speaking personally, completely shared Rentis's hope that the Greek-Bulgarian 'incident, rather than the Corfu settlement, would be the precedent by which such cases would in future be regulated'.[65] In this hope both Rentis and Lampson were, of course, to be disappointed.

The question of deducting the indemnity to be paid by Greece to Bulgaria from Bulgarian war reparation payments to Greece was not dead, at least as far as the Greeks were concerned, and was raised again by General Pangalos and the Greek Foreign Minister, Roufos, the following day in Athens. The Greek Government, Pangalos explained to Cheetham, had definitely decided, and without any reservation, to accept the Council's decision. This would be done, despite the fact that Greece's prestige would be considerably injured and the risk to his country of further political division and unrest. He contended, however, that Greece was not in a position to pay Bulgaria the indemnity within the two-month period prescribed. Pangalos desired, therefore, to appeal to the British Government and referred to the suggestion made previously that the indemnity to be paid should be set off against reparation payments due to Greece, in accordance with a rule of equity recently adopted by the Allies in the case of Greece's war debts.[66] A similar plea was also made by Roufos in a note to Cheetham which also raised the point that the Council's decision on this question would work for peace in the Balkans within the framework of the existing treaties.[67] In forwarding this information to London, Cheetham noted that Greek finances were not in good shape, payment of claims was being deferred wherever this was possible, and money was owed to the Refugee Commission working in Greece.[68] On the following day, 16 December, the Greek delegation also raised the question in a note to the League Council, but were informed by the Council's Italian President, Scialoja, that the

[65] Record of a Conversation between Mr. Lampson and Mr. Rentis, 14 Dec. 1925. File 13309, FO/371/10673, PRO.
[66] Athens to the F.O., no. 222, 16 Dec. 1925. File 953, FO/286/916, PRO.
[67] Roufos to Cheetham, no. 1803, 15 Dec. 1925. French Text. File 953, FO/286/916, PRO.
[68] Sir M.C. to the F.O., no. 224, 15 Dec. 1925. File 953, FO/286/916, PRO.

Council's position had already been made known to Greece, and the delegation's attention was drawn to the terms of the Council's report.[69]

Despite the negative attitude previously displayed towards this Greek proposal, it was nevertheless referred once more to the British Treasury for an opinion. Replying on the same day that he received the request from the Foreign Office, 22 December, Sir Frederick Leith-Ross, the Deputy-Controller of Finance, wrote that he had laid the Greek proposal before the Treasury's Lords Commissioners and was requested to inform Chamberlain that the proposal was 'open to considerable objections' for reasons that Sir Otto Niemeyer had already mentioned in his communication to Lampson on 8 December. The effect of the Greek proposal would be to postpone for an extended period of time the immediate payment of the indemnity. The Lords Commissioners therefore suggested that Athens be informed that its proposal could only be considered if it were presented with the assent of the Bulgarian authorities. Lastly, the Lords Commissioners did not consider that the suggestion contained in Cheetham's communication, that Greece was 'unable to find funds to meet the payment due to Bulgaria, [was] one that [could] be seriously maintained'.[70]

On the last day of the year Lampson communicated Leith-Ross's message to Cheetham in Athens. He explained to Cheetham the Greek efforts made in London and Geneva in the early part of the month to have the Greek proposal accepted. The League Secretariat, however, had not been favourably inclined and its decision had also been seconded by Sir Horace Rumbold, to whom the Greek proposal had also been mentioned. The Secretariat felt that if the indemnity to Bulgaria was to serve any useful purpose, it should be paid by Greece immediately and that delay would complicate the situation and give rise to questions which the Council was not in a position to deal with. Moreover, the Secretariat believed that there was no connection between the reparation arising from the destruction caused during the war and the damage arising from the frontier incident. There was also the question, Lampson continued, that the Greek proposal would have to be considered by the Reparations Commission sitting in Paris and this would have en-

[69] Lampson to Cheetham, 31 Dec. 1925. File 953, FO/286/916, PRO.
[70] A note by Frederick Leith-Ross, 22 Dec. 1925. File 953, FO/286/916, PRO.

tailed delay and helped to negate the object of the indemnity, which was to see that the sufferings caused by the Greek invasion should be alleviated as quickly as possible. The League Secretariat's attitude, therefore, was that the indemnity should take the form of a cash payment within a fixed time limit. The British delegation, he further explained, had also considered the financial aspects of the Greek proposal, and he enclosed for Cheetham a copy of Niemeyer's memorandum.

The Greek proposal, Lampson noted, had not been mentioned before Chamberlain's subcommittee until 11 December. On that day, Hymans, the Belgian, had asked whether such a suggestion was feasible. Lampson had replied that such a proposal might be discussed, but that it was preferable that it should not be, since there was a distinction to be made between an indemnity arising out of a frontier incident and reparation arising out of the war. The League Council was not competent to deal with questions arising out of war reparation, and the Reparations Commission in Paris, the only competent body, might reject such an arrangement as proposed by the Greeks. To connect indemnity with reparation would merely complicate an otherwise clear situation. Lampson had also repeated to Hymans the need for the Bulgarians to compensate quickly those who had suffered from the Greek invasion. He also found it hard to believe that Greece could not find the sum needed to pay the Bulgarians their indemnity, and drew Hymans's attention to the fact that the Athens government was usually able to find money from its revenue for armaments. Lampson's words appeared to satisfy Hymans and he did not press the matter further. In the end the Council stipulated that the Greeks should pay the indemnity within two months.

The fixed time limit ruled out any arrangement such as that proposed by the Greeks. The report adopted by the League Council was accepted by the Greeks and the Bulgarians without any reservations. Thus there was no reason to consider the Greek proposal further. In these circumstances there was no useful purpose to be served by Cheetham reverting to the topic in discussions with the Pangalos government, unless it specifically mentioned the proposal to him. If this were done, Cheetham was to make it clear that the British Government could not agree to entertaining the proposal for the reasons that Lampson had already made clear. At the same time Cheetham was to indicate that the question was one which primarily concerned the League Council; it did not directly concern the British Government or any other government represented on the Council.[71]

It appears that the Greeks pushed their proposal no further. The new year arrived, and on 15 February 1926, almost two months from the day of the Council's decision, the Bulgarian chargé d'affaires in Bern informed Drummond that the Greeks had paid half the sum due, the other half to be paid on 1 March. This delay in payment, the Greeks explained, was necessitated by their difficult financial situation. The Bulgarian Government agreed to this arrangement in order to give 'further proof of its good-will'. The Greek payment of the other half of the indemnity in March brought the Greek-Bulgarian Incident to a close.[72]

The League Council's success as an organ of international coercion had been due to a unique combination of factors which would never occur again in the years that were to follow; and unfortunately, the precedent, which many thought had been established, was never to be repeated.

[71] Lampson to Cheetham, no. 782, 31 Dec. 1925. File 953, FO/286/916, PRO.
[72] League of Nations, *Official Journal*, 7th year, 1925, pp. 584–5.

CONCLUSIONS

THE difference between the Covenant of the League of Nations and all previous attempts at international organization lay in its provisions for collective security. This aspect of the world organization strongly appealed to people of goodwill and was often cited to justify the very establishment of the organization.

To many, collective security was attractive because it seemed a great improvement on the apparently anarchic system of alliances and coalitions which had flourished previously, and was viewed by many as largely responsible for the First World War. It was argued that since collective security was directed against no specific power, it was friendly to all, especially the weak. However, as the memoranda in the appendices by Sir Arthur Salter and Dr. Joost Adrian van Hamel clearly show, there were difficulties in implementing the League's collective security arrangements; difficulties that stimulated discussion during the Greek-Bulgarian Incident and caused hardships during the Ethiopian Crisis, a decade later.

Though collective security was the most important feature of the League and its weapon of last resort, the organization attempted in practice to circumscribe and restrict the traditional right of a state to resort to war—a right which prior to the First World War was perfectly legal under accepted norms of international law. The actions and procedures of the League thus resembled regulations rather than interdictions. It attempted to limit a nation's right to make war by compelling initial recourse to the measures of pacific settlement stipulated in the Covenant: arbitration, conciliation, and judicial settlement.

It should be borne in mind that the founders of the League of Nations did not establish a super-state; they established by treaty a super-association. The basic unit of organization in the League—as in the United Nations—was the state, which did not surrender one iota of its sovereignty. The League organization was not established to change the world. Its primary task was to make the League machinery for peaceful settlement readily available to all nations; secondly, it was to assist nations in the task of achieving peaceful settlement; finally, by the creation of permanent rather than *ad hoc* institutions for peaceful change, it was to help build a system of international co-operation, and so maintain the peace of the world.

The underlying assumption, however, on which this whole edifice for peaceful settlement rested, was that all nations—and particularly the Great Powers—would be willing and anxious to use the machinery of the League in disputes involving them directly. They would do this because they would be following disinterested foreign policies in which nations were guided by community interests rather than considerations of power. In actual practice, though nations realized the value and possibilities of co-operation through the League of Nations and attempted, whenever possible, to integrate the world organization into their policies, they did not do this at the expense of what they considered their vital national interests. Unfortunately, the feeling of a world community during the interwar years was too abstract to warrant sacrifices for nations close by or far away. This feeling was particularly noticeable when discussions in the Council and Assembly of the League centred round the problem of applying the organization's enforcement machinery against an aggressor state. In these discussions, unless the interests of the powers—and especially the Great Powers—coincided, unless there was a direct and immediate interest among the major powers to thwart an aggressor state, League action was doomed to failure.

The League was a Great Power monopoly. This was mirrored in the Council of the League, which was intended to act as the executive organ of the organization. There the Great Powers were entitled to permanent representation, an advantage codified in the Covenant and enjoyed by no other states. Yet permanent Great Power representation was realistic, for it recognized their influence on the world scene. It was also in keeping with the historical experience of Europe, which, from the Congress of Vienna until the eve of the First World War, had been dominated by the Concert of Powers—a euphemism for the dictatorship of the Great Powers.

Thus, when the co-operation of the Great Powers was not forthcoming, decisive action against any nation proved virtually impossible. The requirement that substantive Council action be unanimous only increased the difficulties of the world organization and made the agreement of the Great Powers imperative.

The League could therefore be no more successful than the Great Powers were willing to make it. If there were disagreement among the Great Powers outside the League, it would almost automatically be reflected within the organization. The realization that no international organization established along League lines could be successful unless it possessed the consensus of the Great Powers was formalized in the Security Council of the United Nations by the unanimity rule of Article 27 of the Charter. Under that well-known article, a negative vote by a permanent member is sufficient to thwart Council action on any substantive issue. In a sense, Security Council voting procedure is an improvement over the League Council's, since it limits the veto only to the Great Powers, whereas in the League Council it was a right held by all members. If the Security Council's role is one of maintaining the peace, this voting procedure was a tacit admission at San Francisco that the world organization could not be effective against a Great Power, but only against small states unallied to any Great Power or power bloc.

The Corfu Incident of 1923 was the first occasion on which it became clear that the League could not operate successfully without the agreement of the Great Powers. Mussolini's bombardment and occupation of this defenceless Greek island found Anglo-French policy divided. Though the English were willing to bring the matter to the Council, the French were not. The feeling in the Quai d'Orsay was that if the Greek appeal over Corfu could be allowed to come to the League Council, a precedent would perhaps be established for a German appeal concerning the French occupation of the Ruhr, an occupation which had begun in January, that year. Subsequent realization by the British that they were militarily over-extended in the Mediterranean, plus the rejection of Foreign Office overtures in Paris for a joint British-French naval demonstration, forced Whitehall to compromise the issue outside the League.[1]

The Greek-Bulgarian Incident therefore offers an excellent contrast to this, as well as an insight into the possibilities of collective security and peaceful settlement under the League of Nations, and international organizations in general. The elements lacking in the Corfu Incident for the collective action of the Great Powers, and found in the Greek-Bulgarian Incident, were two: first, the nations directly involved in the Greek-Bulgarian dispute were merely minor powers in the configuration of European politics. Economically,

---

[1] James Barros, *The Corfu Incident of 1923: Mussolini and the League of Nations* (Princeton University Press, 1965).

Greece was reeling under the impact of more than a million refugees who had flooded the country after the exchange of populations with Turkey, agreed to at the Lausanne Conference several years before. Politically, the country was seething with unrest as a result of the dictatorial government of General Pangalos. Though these conditions help in part to explain the Greek decision to obey the Great Powers, undoubtedly the most important consideration was its military weakness and susceptibility to naval blockade and harassment, a condition that the decision-makers in Athens did not lose sight of. Similarly, a demilitarized, friendless, and isolated Bulgaria was more than happy to comply with any and all requests made by the Great Powers. The fact that neither nation was tied to one of the Great Powers in any alliance, formal or informal, expedited the task of the powers and made collective action possible.

Secondly, and perhaps most important, the signature of the Locarno Pacts by all the Great Powers, only days before the incident erupted, provided that immediate and direct interest which was so important in galvanizing and co-ordinating the action of the Great Powers. The desire to consolidate the new European *status quo*, legalized by the Locarno settlement, and make sure that no action by any state jeopardize this settlement, drove all the powers to act in unison and with dispatch.

This can certainly be the only explanation for Briand's quick actions, both as Foreign Minister and Acting President of the League Council. His actions are of even greater significance, if one keeps in mind that to the French, the League was viewed as only one more instrument among many others, to be used against any future German menace, and that French interests inevitably began to lapse when discussions of sanctions against a nation other than Germany took place.[2]

The same may be said of the actions of Sir Austen Chamberlain and his hurried return to Paris, only days after his triumphal return from Locarno. It was an action out of step with British views of the League, which, after the American Senate's rejection of the Covenant, looked upon the organization as a sort of great world debating society where nations might meet to air their grievances, rather than as an organ for political settlement.[3] Like the French and British,

[2] Arnold Wolfers, *Britain and France between Two Wars* (Harcourt, Brace and Co., 1940).
[3] Ibid.

the Italians also saw greater advantage in the united action of the Great Powers than in allowing a dangerous situation to develop which might jeopardize the Locarno settlement. Though Italy had never been one of the League's most enthusiastic supporters, Mussolini was willing to act jointly through the world organization which only two years before, during the Corfu Incident, he had openly flouted. The fact that Italian actions would in the long run assist Bulgaria, a country with which Mussolini was attempting to establish closer relations, made the Italian decision undoubtedly easier.

The Great Powers applied direct pressure with increasing intensity to both sides, and this policy was later continued by using the machinery of the world organization. Such pressure would, in the long run, as Sir Austen Chamberlain saw, be sufficient to make the Greeks succumb to the desires of the powers. The avoidance of sanctions imposed through the League of Nations, as desired by Sir Austen, was probably for the best, for the application of sanctions and force against the Greeks posed dangers for the League at this time. Legal and political problems of the first order would have had to be faced—if one is to judge from the conversations of the British Cabinet—during a period when the League was still trying, after its failure in the Corfu Incident two years before, to establish itself as a viable instrument for peaceful settlement.

In passing, the activities of the Secretary-General, Sir Eric Drummond, as well as other members of the Secretariat should also be noted. From the beginning of the incident, as we have seen, the Secretary-General, took a very active role behind the scenes in attempting to influence the actions of the British, and in moderating those of the Greek Government. As a British citizen and former member of the British Foreign Office, Drummond was in a unique position to attempt the former, and his role as Secretary-General gave him the opportunity to attempt the latter. These initiatives by Drummond are extremely interesting, since the position of Secretary-General under the Covenant of the League of Nations was far less political than under the Charter of the United Nations. Even though Sir Eric's appeals were ignored in Athens, and anticipated in London, his initiatives clearly show that, provided the Secretary-General is aware of the limits of his power, he can play an important and active role in the world organization. The problem arises, however, that it often becomes difficult to ascertain when the Secretary-General is acting as an international official of a world organization, and when he is acting as a national of his own country. This blurring of function and nationality was clearly evident in the Secretariat during the settlement of the incident if the actions of Major Abraham and of Aghnides are examined. On the whole Drummond was quite aware of his limited powers and accordingly, in the Greek-Bulgarian Incident as well as in other situations, he astutely and discreetly used his position and the prestige of his office to tender advice and to act as a mediator.[4]

The discretion of a Drummond, however, who, apart from his first years as Secretary-General, served the League during a comparatively peaceful period, was not to be repeated by his successor, the Frenchman, Joseph Avenol. Avenol's activities and initiatives during the seven crucial years of 1933–40 helped to exacerbate the tensions of the world community, and went a long way in damaging the political, not to speak of the moral, position of the world organization. His use of the office raises the question of whether political initiatives undertaken by a Secretary-General without authorization or close supervision are desirable, and whether the good that can be achieved by a Secretary-General in world affairs is more than offset by the damage that he can cause.[5]

It would appear from this investigation of the Greek-Bulgarian Incident that, provided the Great Powers can agree to act collectively because of mutual interests, pressure to achieve peaceful settlement can and will be applied by the Great Powers. If diplomatic pressure proves insufficient, direct physical pressure will be considered and inevitably supplied, either within or outside the organization. But this situation leads to certain questions, for if collective action by the powers is a tenuous proposition at best, why institutionalize it within international organization at all? Are not greater risks presented by keeping it within the structure of the organization? For example, if collective action is institutionalized and unable to operate because of disagreement between the Great Powers out-

[4] Though Sir Eric Drummond (subsequently Lord Perth) proved an extremely effective Secretary-General behind the scenes, he was less successful when he left the League and served as Ambassador to Rome. Felix Gilbert, 'Two British Ambassadors: Perth and Henderson', in Craig and Gilbert (eds.), *The Diplomats 1919–1939* (Princeton University Press, 1953), pp. 537–54; Anthony Eden, *Facing the Dictators; the Memoirs of Anthony Eden, Earl of Avon* (Houghton Mifflin, 1962).

[5] James Barros, *Betrayal from Within: Joseph Avenol, Secretary-General of the League of Nations, 1933–1940* (Yale University Press, 1969).

side the organization, causing a paralysis of the organization, does not the organization's prestige decrease, and disillusionment set in? Do not these adverse reactions in turn hinder, if not destroy, the attempt to construct an atmosphere in which peaceful change may prove possible, especially through the procedures established by the organization? Some reply that even the few successful actions undertaken through the world organization help to establish a tradition making international coercion legitimate, and accordingly the coercive aspects should be maintained as an integral part of any international organization.

Perhaps in the League, and for that matter in the United Nations, it would have been better to have restricted the organization's jurisdiction only to social and economic fields of endeavour, until such time as the actions of the powers, the feelings for a world community, and the desire for co-operation, would permit a greater assumption of responsibility by the organization. By tackling and solving economic and social problems, considered by many to contribute largely to the tensions that rack the international community, the organization could help to produce an atmosphere in which expansion of its powers might take place. At the same time the organization could still play an important political role, being the meeting-ground where competing states might always make contact. None of this would preclude the world organization's acting as an organ for conciliation and mediation where its actions are merely a recommendation and have no binding force on the parties involved —as was the case in the League and is today in the United Nations. Indeed, it would appear from recent examinations of both the League's and the United Nations' endeavours in this sphere that the conciliatory and mediatory procedures of a world organization offer nations a means of escape from internal domestic pressures on certain issues of foreign policy which, if allowed to fester, could lead to both internal and external crises.[6]

By divorcing itself from the coercive aspects, the organization would be removing itself from an area of conflict which experience shows is unlikely to be settled by international organization, unless the Great Powers collaborate. In situations where the Great Powers

[6] The questions examined were fortuitously insular. James Barros, *The Aland Islands Question: Its Settlement by the League of Nations* (Yale University Press, 1968) and Stephen G. Xydis, *Cyprus: Conflict and Conciliation, 1954–1958* (Ohio State University Press, 1967).

can agree outside the organization, the organization appears to serve no necessary function and becomes superfluous. Coercive measures, and these may include peace-keeping missions, when forced through the organization by procedural or constitutional manipulations, cause a greater increase of tensions in the world community and a feeling of malevolence towards the organization itself, since these actions are considered by one side as an attempt by the other to legitimatize its actions under the aegis of the organization. On the other hand, an organization narrower in scope is not harmed if there is disagreement by the Great Powers outside the organization.

The assumptions made at Paris in 1919 about the value of international organization as a political instrument within international politics were never seriously questioned at San Francisco in 1945. Yet experience seems to show that there might be greater advantages in keeping the purview of international organization narrow in scope, rather than broad. Though the Greek-Bulgarian Incident, because of the collective action of the Great Powers, increased the prestige of the League of Nations, the subsequent disagreement of the Great Powers outside the League was reflected within the organization, especially in important political episodes like Manchuria, or the Chaco War between Paraguay and Bolivia, as well as in the Ethiopian debacle, causing the organization a great loss of prestige and effectiveness as an organ for coercion and peaceful settlement.

These episodes had been preceded by discussions within the British Foreign Office which went a long way to undermine the precedent established by the League in its settlement of the Greek-Bulgarian Incident. In late September of 1931, six years after the incident had been brought to a peaceful and successful conclusion, China appealed to the League Council on the question of Japan's invasion of Manchuria. The Chinese appeal provoked discussion within the British Foreign Office, sparked off by Douglas MacKillop, of the Far Eastern Department, who interestingly enough had served in Greece from 1926 to 1928. Referring to China's appeal to the League Council, MacKillop noted that since each dispute differed, was 'it established for all time that the appeal to be made by the League Council to the disputants [was] merely to be varied on points of *form* from the locus classicus of the Greco-Bulgarian dispute, and that the *substance* of the policy and procedure to be adopted by the League [was] to remain determined by that precedent'? If this was so, MacKillop thought it was 'a very dangerous doctrine to apply to a dispute between a foreign power and China'. According to MacKillop, parties to a dispute differed, as did disputes. China was neither Bulgaria nor Greece. If Great Britain, he asked, had a dispute with China (as London always had, either actually in existence or at any rate in the offing) was the British delegate to the League to say that Great Britain must withdraw its troops from Shanghai and the British fleet from Chinese waters? The position regarding the maintenance of military forces in China was, MacKillop pointed out, defined in a resolution adopted at the Washington Conference on the Limitation of Armament. Britain's policy towards China was based entirely on the instruments and resolutions of this conference. It was clear, MacKillop continued, that, 'in this respect as in so many others China [was] *sui generis* and the principles applicable to disputes between states in general do not by any means necessarily apply to disputes between China and another state'. It followed that Great Britain had to allow a friendly state—in this case Japan—to act towards China in a different way from how it would allow Japan to act towards another state, since Great Britain itself treated China in a different manner, 'consciously and constantly'.[7]

MacKillop's minute, which was essentially an argument that the precedent established in 1925 was not applicable to China in general and to the Manchurian question in particular, was not in line with Chamberlain's comments to Rentis at Geneva in December 1925. What it, in fact, meant was that the precedent established was to be applied only when necessary, and obviously necessity would be dictated by national interests and subjective considerations, none of which would contribute to developing objective universal norms for state behaviour which the precedent was intended to establish.

Within the Foreign Office one of MacKillop's colleagues minuted: 'I agree. Hard and fast principles are dangerous'. To this comment the Permanent Under-Secretary, Sir Robert Vansittart, also penned his agreement.[8] The last comment, however, was interestingly enough made by Anthony Eden, the young and newly appointed Parliamentary Under-Secretary of State for Foreign

---

[7] Minute by D. MacKillop, 30 Sept. 1931. File 1391, FO/371/15490, PRO.

[8] Minute by Sir R.V. and another attached minute whose signature is illegible, 30 Sept. 1931. File 1391, FO/371/15490, PRO.

Affairs. He likewise agreed. Eden believed that there was 'real danger in pressing the only available precedent too far. The Greco-Bulgarian dispute bears no truer analogy to the Manchurian troubles', he wrote, 'than it would to any accentuation of our difficulties with China. The League is always tempted naturally enough, to press precedents unduly where these are inevitably few. The consequences may serve the immediate ends of the Council, but not so certainly meet the canons of equity'.[9]

These Foreign Office comments, which clearly contradicted Chamberlain's words at Geneva in December 1925, show that an international organization like the League or the United Nations can be no more effective as an instrument of peace than the nations using it wish it to be. How they use or misuse the organ will to a large extent decide the effectiveness of the organ. The proper appreciation of an institution like the League or the United Nations depends on first realizing its limitations in a world dominated by power. To view international organization in any other light is to be short-sighted about the realities of the international community, where power is the omnipresent weapon of all states and particularly the great.

[9] Minute by A.E., 6 Oct. 1931. File 1391, FO/371/15490, PRO.

APPENDIX A

THE GRECO-BULGAR INCIDENT

'SANCTIONS'[1]

9 November 1925

AT one stage of the Greco-Bulgar incident, it looked as if some means of pressure might have to be found by the Council. It seems likely that (had the pressure required been against Greece) the Council would have wished to invite the Governments of Great Britain, France, and Italy to send ships off to Athens, this naval demonstration being accompanied or followed by the withdrawal of ministers by both these and other member states. This possibility led to unofficial discussions as to the form, and legal authority, under which, if the need arose, such action should be taken.

As the type of case illustrated in this incident may well recur, I think it worthwhile to put on record the views recorded with some comments.

(1) It was urged on the one hand that any measures involving real pressure, and in particular such a measure as the arrangement of a naval demonstration should only be taken under Article 16, the only article authorizing sanctions and that therefore the proposed action should be specifically based on this article. It was argued in support of this that the right of the Council, under Article 10 to 'advise upon the means by which this obligation (that of respecting and preserving territorial integrity and political independence) shall be fulfilled', was only meant to cover measures short of sanctions, such as consultation between governments and the exercise of diplomatic pressure. The same argument was applied to Article 11 which, in case of war or threat of war, prescribes that the League shall 'take any action that may be deemed wise and effectual to safeguard the peace of nations'.

The objections to this view seemed to be the following:

(*a*) At the stage at which pressure might have been required the Council might have found it difficult, and considered it impolitic, to declare that there had been 'resort to war'. Doubtless Greece would have committed acts which Bulgaria might, on the ordinary principles of international law, have considered acts of hostility justifying resistance, which would have entailed war. But in the absence of such resistance it

---

[1] Political 1925, League of Nations Archives.

would have involved an important decision of principle to state that there had been 'resort to war' (cf. Corfu case). Such a decision might in certain circumstances be necessary, but the Council would probably hesitate to take it in the first instance at a stage at which it desired to take no measures more drastic than the arrangement of a naval demonstration.

(b) In my view an even more serious objection is to be found in the fact that a declaration that there had been 'resort to war' and that therefore Article 16 was in force accompanied only by a naval demonstration, or that plus the withdrawal of ministers, would have amounted to an implied abrogation of the specific and unconditional obligation falling directly upon all members under Article 16 to sever, in such a case, 'all trade and financial relations', etc.

Now it may well be that, in applying Article 16 when the time arrives the Council may have to modify, retard, and adjust the application of the sanctions in accordance with the indications of the 1921 Assembly Resolution or otherwise.

But to take a decision at once implying the abrogation of the direct obligation, as an incident to the application of so simple a measure as a naval demonstration and without prolonged and careful consideration of the consequences on the vital Article 16, would surely have been open to the greatest objection.

(2) The gravity of this objection is illustrated by a suggestion made by one member of the Council that economic sanctions were extremely expensive and onerous and that, if sanctions were required, military and naval action would be preferable.

If by this was meant only a naval demonstration, the suggestion is sufficiently dealt with in the rest of this note. But if what he had in mind was more than this, i.e. that if the demonstration were insufficient the subsequent action should be, e.g., bombardment, without the general severance of economic relations, the following comments must be made.

(a) It seems contrary to the whole spirit of the Covenant, and especially Article 16, that military action in this sense should precede, and be accompanied by, general economic sanctions. The whole suggestion of the Covenant is 'do what you can by economic pressure; supplement if necessary by military action'.

(b) Apart from the intentions of the Covenant the political importance of giving priority to economic pressure can hardly be overestimated: particularly as regards the U.S.A. and Great Britain.

(c) Apart from the general political advantage of economic pressure, there is this special consideration. Military or naval action means usually the action of one or two powers. The objection to 'giving the British Navy to the League', etc., would be immensely strengthened if the Navy were asked to take such drastic action as bombardment, while other member states were not asked to suffer the economic loss involved in the stoppage of trade. Moreover the moral authority behind such action would be much less. Action would be much more 'Great Power action'; it would weaken the character of the League itself as an organ of collective, and as far as possible equal world authority.

(3) It was again suggested that the naval demonstration might be made under the powers of Article 10. 'The Council shall advise upon the means by which this obligation (to respect and preserve against external aggression territorial integrity and political independence) shall be fulfilled'.

Greek troops were at the time undeniably in Bulgarian territory and the immediate object of the pressure would have been to secure their withdrawal. The action would therefore appear to be specially relevant to the duty of preserving against external aggression. At the same time there were, in my view, the following objections to this course.

(a) Article 10 is the most ambiguous, the most contested, and has been the most politically important of all articles in the Covenant. It is specially important not to give it more than its uncontested meaning as an incident to action that could be properly based on other articles. I refer especially to the following ambiguities.

(b) Is it clear that 'political integrity' is exactly the same as 'political inviolability'? Does it necessarily mean more than that member states undertake that annexation shall not be secured by aggression (i.e. that they will see that the terms of peace involve restoration of territory)? Now there was no suggestion in this case that annexation was intended.

(c) Is it not at least a tenable view that the principle of preserving political territory having been posed in Article 10, we must look to the subsequent articles to define the application of this principle? Can we not conceive a case for example in which, a dispute having taken place, the procedure of Article 15 having been followed, the Council having been not unanimous, it would remain open to a member without breach of the Covenant to take military action which would ultimately result in interfering with political integrity. Does Article 10 necessarily override the provisions as to the 'gap' for freedom of action?

I am not arguing as to which view is right. But is there not room for difference of opinion?

(d) There remain the arguments stated in (1) above as to the limited character of the 'means' contemplated in Article 10. I do not myself follow this argument so far as to think they would (if there were no other difficulties) exclude such action as a naval demonstration (see note as to Article 11 under 4 below), but they are worth bearing in mind.

(4) Another suggestion, for which in my view the case is much stronger, was that the proposed action should be taken under Article 11. 'Any war or threat of war . . . is hereby declared a matter of concern to the whole League, and the League shall take any action that may be

deemed wise and effectual to safeguard the peace of nations. In case any such emergency should arise, the S[ecretary]-G[eneral] shall on the request of any member of the League forthwith summon a meeting of the Council.'

It was under this article that the Council was summoned. Indubitably a threat of war existed. The phrase 'any action, etc.', is wide. As to the arguments under (1) above, it is difficult to say that so wide a phrase would not justify so restricted a measure as a naval demonstration.

At the same time a naval demonstration in its essence is a threat of the possibility of something more—what is the 'something more'? I think, indubitably, in view of the considerations under (2) above, it should in the first instance have been economic pressure, not bombardment. I thought it would be well to suggest this in the original formula (see 6 below).

But would even economic pressure be justified under Article 11 alone? Personally I am inclined to think at any rate the most drastic would not. I believe there is *some* validity in the argument under (1). I believe the natural and reasonable interpretation of 'any action' under Article 11, in the context of the rest of the Covenant, is 'any action short of such action as in the case of an individual member of the League would constitute an act of war or a resort to war'. I think that, if the Council desires action of this kind to be taken, it should take it under Article 16 and would only be justified in taking it if it felt able to say that the condition on which Article 16 comes into force that there had been resort to war—was fulfilled.

In other words I think a naval demonstration (which in itself is not equivalent to a resort to war and is indeed not an act of war) would be justified under Article 11, and is best taken under that article, but that inasmuch as it is a menace of something more and that 'something more' could only be taken under Article 16, the original formula should contain a reference to Article 16 (see 6 below).

(5) Yet another suggestion was made: that the Council should act under the 'general powers entrusted to it in the Covenant' without specifying any particular article or articles. The idea behind this proposal is that the Council should build up its powers by precedent and case-law, which would be recognized as such by the Court of Justice, thus securing greater elasticity than is given by the written law of the Covenant.

I think this is a dangerous and very objectionable proposal for the following reasons:

(a) I think it is scarcely credible that it would be proposed if the aggressor were a Great Power. The Council would in such a case certainly feel bound to base its action on a specific right contained in a definite text.

(b) The conception is very distinctively British and non-continental.

(*c*) It reflects and would tend to develop the conception of the League as a 'European Concert', the Great Powers dominating the others and developing their own policy and rights. The rights of the small Powers depend on the sanctity of the written text.

(6) The suggestion which I think the best results almost automatically from the above arguments. It is as follows:

'In virtue of the provisions of the Covenant, in particular those of articles [10 and] 11, and in view of the possibility of action under Article 16 being necessary at an early date, the Council invites the Governments of Great Britain, France and Italy to send ships of war to the proximity of the ports of Piraeus and Phalerum (but, pending further instructions, with due respect for territorial waters), in order that they may be in a position, if the necessity arises, to assist in the application of the economic sanctions which the Council may recommend in accordance with Article 16'.

On the whole I would prefer (for the reasons given under 3) to omit the words in square brackets, though I am a little uncertain on this. And on the whole I would prefer to retain the words in brackets, though here again with some hesitation. The operation might be technically difficult— there might be difficulties of anchorage for example. But if practicable, there is some advantage in the Council only advising action, until it is prepared to say that Article 16 is in force, of a kind which, by the recognized principles of international law, a country could take without committing a hostile or questionable act.

(7) Turning now from the formula to policy. I think the best further action for the Council to have taken in addition to the above decision would have been:

(*a*) Simultaneously with the decision, to send the decision to all member states warning them of the possibility that they may soon be called upon to co-operate in the application of the provisions of Article 16 if the need should arise, and indicating that the Council would in that case continue its deliberations and communicate with them again.

It might have been well at the same time to communicate the decision formally to non-member states (see 7(*e*) below).

(*b*) If the demonstration were not immediately effective simultaneous withdrawal of all Ministers of all Council States and so far as possible all other member states (the Legation staffs, however, remaining). Neutral states, particularly U.S.A., might have been invited to associate themselves in this action.

(*c*) Council makes definite blockade plans, inviting adjacent countries; appoints Blockade Advisory Council, but as to immediate practical action concentrates especially on *close sea blockade of Athens and its ports, Phalerum and Piraeus*, the remaining measures of economic pressure being applied gradually and with increasing stringency.

(8) The advantages of the above procedure are:

(*a*) It would avoid any action legally disputable.

(*b*) Measures involving serious loss would only be taken if absolutely necessary.

(*c*) It would secure the maximum of collective moral authority.

(*d*) The pressure on Athens, whose population would first see the combined fleet, and then, if necessary, directly suffer the loss of imports, would be rapid and overwhelming.

(*e*) There is one more advantage of the greatest importance. The great difficulty of effective blockade is the uncertainty as to America's action. It is difficult for a country like Great Britain to take at once definite action such as the institution of a naval blockade, without knowing whether she will soon be faced with the dilemma of either stopping American ships under serious protests or going back on her decision. An answer from America on a purely hypothetical case could probably not be obtained. But if ships were sent with a clear indication in the decision that, if necessary, the first action would be to institute a close blockade of a defined area, we should know the American attitude before taking the decisive step. And, what is equally important, we should have established conditions which would be favourable. The close blockade offers the least of difficulties from the point of view of international law and the American view of it. The nature of the dispute, the moral authority of the collective League decision, the character of the action immediately prepared would make it certain that, at the worst, the American attitude would be 'we are a neutral, as a neutral we recognize the validity of blockade so established': it would be likely indeed to be more favourable and include a definite expression of goodwill if not actual co-operation. But even the first of these would be an immense reinforcement and a source of additional strength for the future.

(Initialled) J. A. S[alter]

APPENDIX B

SANCTIONS[1]

17 November 1925

(1) I have read Salter's paper with the greatest interest. It is extremely useful that, as a consequence of the Greco-Bulgarian incident, we in the Secretariat should be led to give account of possible action with regard to sanctions. The present round-the-table talk on paper may be very helpful for this purpose.

Salter's paper contains most valuable suggestions and on several points our conclusions are more similar than I thought at first. It may not be impossible to establish, perhaps with a few exceptions, a common doctrine. I should be glad if Salter and other officials to whom these papers are submitted will consider the various observations now set forth.

(2) As far as sanctions are concerned, a distinction should be made between matters for which the Council can call upon Members and in which their participation is *obligatory*—and others in which the Council can avail itself of the *voluntary* participation of certain members.

Action *obligatory* on individual members can only be based on Article 16 of the Covenant.

Apart from this, *voluntary* action may be based on other articles. In the present instance, Articles 10 and 11 come up for consideration. In other cases, the last part of Article 13 might come into play.

I therefore come to the conclusion that in no case where the Council calls upon members to fulfil an *obligation* of collective action for sanctions under the Covenant, should it do so under any article other than Article 16; but, on the other hand, the Council may find it desirable to organize, always under its authority, special action to which members would not be obliged, but for which the Council can invite specific members.

I will come back to the question of the desirability of always keeping very clearly in view this distinction between action *obligatory* on the individual members and the organization of *voluntary* action.

(3) In cases like the present, the initial action of the League should be based on Articles 10 and 11. With regard to Salter's draft (no. 6 of his memorandum) on this point I would propose *not* to omit the words in square brackets.

---

[1] Political 1925, League of Nations Archives.

Article 11 certainly forms a basis for general action.

The importance of Article 10 should, however, not be overlooked, particularly in regard to the principle expressed in it. There is no doubt that in certain quarters this Article has met with much criticism. This criticism has, however, been to a very large extent based on misunderstanding and misrepresentation. It is, as far as I can see, gradually dying out; and, on the other hand, in a good many quarters Article 10 continues to be considered as one of the foundation stones of the League: namely, in as far as it is solemnly directed against any interference by violence with existing territorial states. It is not necessary for the present purpose to recall the controversies about Article 10, the actuality of which controversies is, as I said, dying out. For cases like the one under discussion, the practical importance of Article 10 is that it gives a specific direction to the action, which in general the League can take under Article 11. Under Article 11 it is only said that, in case of threat of war, the League may take 'any action wise and effectual to safeguard the peace'. In acting at the same time under Article 10, the Council will recognize, and should recognize, that in cases of territorial aggression this 'any action' should, in the first place envisage the respect for existing territorial integrity and political independence. In the Greco-Bulgarian case, the Council unconsciously applied that principle in a very distinct manner. Under Article 11 alone, maintenance of a *status quo* could be ordered after an invasion without ordering invading parties to withdraw immediately. Article 10 insists on action definitely based on restoration of territorial rights, as recognized by the Covenant. I should therefore suggest that, if and when the case occurs, Article 10 should be included amongst the articles on which the Council bases its action.

I have made it clear by what was said under the previous number that I am, like Salter, in favour of recommending that the Council's action should always be based on specific articles, and not on a general formula. The scope of the existing articles is sufficiently large to allow the Council to build up its powers by precedent, but, in order not to lay its action open to question by interested powers and in order to be able eventually to defend such action before a legal examination, the legal basis thereof should be clearly indicated.

(4) On the other hand, I could caution against a too narrow—particularly against a too technical—interpretation of various terms used in the Covenant. I found some traces of this tendency in the discussions we had on the subject. If such a tendency be allowed to develop, the League's action may be exposed to ineffectiveness in the more serious cases. The following are instances of what I call overtechnical interpretations of the Covenant.

(*a*) It is asked whether 'invasion of a territory', not with the object of acquisition, but only with a view to temporary occupation or as a coercive measure, falls under 'external aggression of the territorial integrity' of a country, referred to in Article 10.

Now I feel sure that this is a fatal distinction. It leaves it to a hostile power to defend its aggressive action, and thus to exclude League intervention, by saying that this action is not aiming at permanent acquisition. This would in most cases involve very nice and special pleading. Whatever may have been the original intention of Article 10, it certainly expresses now in very clear words that 'territorial integrity should be respected against every external violence', and that is how its ordinary language should be understood. Should the absolute respect for that integrity not have been demanded, under the Covenant, against violence of a more temporary nature, in such cases as the German invasion of Belgium, the Greek invasion now in Bulgaria or in the Austrian occupation in 1914 of Belgrade as a *prise de gage*?

(*b*) The expressions in Article 11 'any war or threat of war' and in Article 16 'resort to war' are sometimes held as restricting the League's action to cases of technical 'war' or 'threat of war', in the sense of the older conceptions of war as a status between two individual states. A few points made in Salter's admirable paper are based on that more technical conception. Now here again the League should adopt a larger sense of the terms. It would not do to declare League action excluded or unjustifiable because the technical 'status of war' or 'threat of war' is not in existence. It may be true that according to the pre-war international law, war is technically impossible without a formal declaration of war, and is excluded by the intentions of an aggressor not to make war but to apply measures that fall short of war. It would, however, be a great mistake to admit that League action should be restricted by such technical conceptions. In the terminology of the Covenant 'war' means, deliberate hostile [or aggressive] violence, and the League could take action under the said articles, even if one of the interested parties should declare that the technical and traditional legal conception of war is not in existence. This was also the view indicated by the Special Jurists' Committee of 1924 and expressed in their reply to the fourth question.

The point is—and a very important point—that, under the League of Nations' regime, various terms of a legal nature acquire a different meaning from that formerly associated with them. They will be governed by new rules, still to be drawn up, but not at all necessarily forming the continuation of older rules existing under the more anarchic regime of the relations between individual states.

(*c*) This last remark would also apply to the application of so called 'rules of war' when applied in a collective action organized by the League. It would also apply to the application of the economic weapon of the League, which is not necessarily governed by the older rules in existence on the subject of blockade. I do not want to go into this matter more deeply now, but I very strongly want to expose the principle that, in this instance, the League will form or reform law, and will not necessarily be bound by older rules which have arisen under quite different circumstances. The League may even hold that the rules of law it will thus be forming, carefully and with due consideration, should be taken into account by non-members. It would not be at all a new feature in international law for certain rules originally established between certain states, to obtain a much wider legal range *vis-à-vis* other countries.

(5) And now with regard to the action to be exercised by the League: I am not at all sure that practically in many cases the most efficient League action would not consist in military (including naval) action, leaving alone for the moment the economic action of entire boycott and blockade. It is obvious that in cases of at first mere local significance—for instance the Greco-Bulgarian incident—it would be very difficult to get the members of the League really to apply at once the economic weapon. As a matter of fact, the economic weapon is one which works better by being kept in store. Prudent League action should in most cases refrain from applying it or from leading up to its application, and thereby showing its weaknesses. On the other hand, it should always be there theoretically organized, and the possibility of its application never be doubted. It is questionable whether it would be workable, even in very serious circumstances where the world might be divided into two camps, but it certainly would not be easily workable on less serious occasions. This may be regretted, but it is so.

For this reason, any interpretation and application of the Covenant, and particularly of Article 16, making it an automatic necessity in the case of League action to apply the first paragraph of Article 16, would be a mistake. I am, therefore, not so much opposed to some clearly avowed military (or naval) action to be organized by the League in cases of local conflicts, as Salter seems to be. I should like to state that in the first place this action should, of course, always strictly remain under the League's (Council's) authority. Moreover, by military or naval action, I would not easily mean bombardment. A naval demonstration such as now contemplated may be very efficacious. It might be followed by a landing of troops, by a military demonstration on land, by the temporary occupation certain parts of a given territory, by the establishment by force of a neutral zone between the two countries, without developing the nature of a bombardment (it would, however, not be legally excluded). There seems to be no objection to organizing military action of this kind, not only with a view to possible economic action, but also with a view to possible coercive military action.

In this respect, I have, after careful study, come to a different conclusion with regard to the League powers under Articles 11 and 16 from the one I was at first inclined to take.

After careful consideration, and studying the original drafts of these articles and authorities, I now feel sure that under these Articles the League can organize coercive military action which may go very far if, in the interest of peace, it is deemed necessary. As long as the Council can rely upon the voluntary assistance of certain powers, Article 16 need not be invoked.

Of course, the Council should always be very careful, as Salter makes clear, to organize the action in such a manner that it does not deteriorate into individual action of certain powers and so that it should keep a League character, and in no case should an individual power feel authorized to act unless covered by a decision of the full Council of the League. Moreover, the Council could in most cases underline the collective character of its plan, by adding an invitation to all members to sever diplomatic relations, withdraw heads of missions, or to take measures of a similar kind.

(6) If under any circumstance Article 16 should be applied, it would have to be done in a very elastic and progressive manner. The terms of the Article itself may be very categoric; there is, however, no doubt that, for instance, the directive rules already laid down by the Assembly lead up to a much more graduated application, and this point should always be kept in view. It may even be desirable to restrict the blockade to a few ports, and not at once pronounce the entire economic boycott. I would in no case see objection to the Council recommending that for the moment the economic action should be put into effect by certain well-described measures, of course entirely reserving the future application of measures on a large scale. The obligation of Article 16 would thereby not be abrogated (as Salter's paper assumes), but graduated in its application.

(7) Reading the draft resolution suggested by Salter (in no. 6, page 7, of his paper) in the light of these observations, I would not think it necessary to restrict the object of the fleet action to the assistance in the eventual application of economic sanctions. I should like to make certain amendments to the proposed text, beginning for instance:

In virtue of the provisions of the Covenant, in particular those of Articles 10 and 11, and in view of the necessity of taking efficient measures to safeguard the peace of nations and to secure respect for the covenants of the League, in view also of the possibility of economic action under Article 16 being necessary at an early date, the Council invites the governments of . . . to send ships of war to the proximity of . . . in order that they may be in a position, if the necessity arrives, to assist in the said action as the Council shall decide or recommend.

(8) Should a line be added:

'Pending further instructions territorial waters shall be duly respected'?

It may be desirable to mention 'respect for territorial waters, pending further instructions', in order to mark the first rather 'inoffensive' nature of the action. On the other hand, I agree with Salter that an absolute respect for territorial waters should, even in this phase, not be required. Perhaps it would be wise to obtain naval advice on this point. From the legal point of view, I should think that 'inoffensive' action as contemplated in the beginning of the League action would permit the entrance into the maritime belt for *nautical* purposes. This is a point on which the League would make its own law. It should in the beginning respect territorial waters as far as *military* purposes are concerned, but may use them for *nautical* purposes. At any rate, this is my *prima facie* opinion, subject to expert naval advice. I should therefore like to add a line as follows: 'Apart from the requirements of navigation and anchorage, territorial waters shall, pending further instructions be duly respected'.

Van Hamel
Director of the Legal Section

APPENDIX C

MEMORANDUM OF THE SECRETARY-GENERAL

TO DR. VAN HAMEL AND MR. SALTER[1]

31 December 1925

I HAVE read these two memoranda with great interest and they certainly are of much value with regard to the different possibilities discussed and views held during the Greco-Bulgar dispute. I do not, however, purpose to comment on them at any length, because I feel that theoretical discussion on possible future action might be largely academic.

Each occasion, in which questions of sanctions arise will present circumstances peculiar to itself, which will therefore require special treatment. There is one point on which I fully concur with both Mr. A. Salter and van Hamel, namely that League action should always be based on specific articles of the Covenant itself.

Apart from this I incline in theory to van Hamel's view rather than with A. Salter's, though I feel bound to make considerable reserve as against his interpretation of Article 10, but as I said above I do not think it desirable to examine all possibilities and theories in order to endeavour to come to definite conclusions which should necessarily shape League action in all future emergencies. I purpose to consider each case on its merits, if and when it arises. There is, however, one general point made by Salter which is worth underlining, namely that in the case of a situation of real peril to world peace the use of the economic weapon in preference to any other is one of the essential bases of the Covenant.

Certainly the founders of the League having the example of the great war in mind intended to organize an economic barrier against future war.

Many people supported the establishment of the League with this general feeling in mind; though it may have died down a little now, it seems likely that under any serious danger of war it would again become very sharp.

(Initialled) E[ric] D[rummond]

[1] Political 1925, League of Nations Archives.

BIBLIOGRAPHICAL NOTE

As the reader has doubtless noted, almost all the material that made this study possible was archival in nature. It was found in a number of widely scattered places. Of the six parties directly involved in the episode, Bulgaria, Great Britain, France, Greece, Italy, and the League of Nations, the papers of four of them have been examined; the exceptions being Bulgaria and France.

The inability to examine Bulgarian archival material was offset by the two reports filed by Sofia with the League of Nations' Commission of Inquiry, describing its initial reactions when the incident erupted and its subsequent moves. These two reports, found in the League archives and used in conjunction with other archival materials, give a clear picture of Bulgaria's actions during the course of the episode. As for France, the inability to examine its archival material was offset by an examination of the papers of the Greek and Italian Foreign Ministries and the British Foreign Office. These archival deposits show with great clarity the moves of the French Government and especially of its Foreign Minister, Aristide Briand.

Of the archival depositories examined, the most important papers were found in the files of the British Foreign Office, kept at the Public Record Office in London. Unfortunately, some of the most important papers dealing with the episode and to be found in the political file, Foreign Office Record Group 371, had been inadvertently destroyed. This loss, however, was made up by examining Foreign Office Record Group 286, the papers of the British Legation in Athens, which had been returned to the Public Record Office. A similar examination of the papers of the legation in Sofia and of the embassies in Berlin, Paris, and Rome proved impossible, since the archives of these diplomatic missions have never been returned to the Public Record Office. Aside from these materials, Sir Austen Chamberlain's political papers in Foreign Office Record Group 800 were also examined, as were his personal and private papers to be found in the University of Birmingham Library. Finally, the minutes of the British Cabinet were utilized by examining Cabinet Record Group 23, also to be found in the Public Record Office.

The above British materials, reinforced by the papers of the Greek and Italian Foreign Ministries examined in Athens and Rome and those of the League of Nations examined in Geneva, fill out the picture. Although the United States and Germany played no active role in this crisis, the papers of the Department of State and those of the German Foreign Ministry, found in the National Archives in Washington, D.C., throw additional light on dark corners and help to verify information mentioned or cited in other archival sources.

The few published works cited in this study, with the exception of the memoirs of the French Minister in Athens, Count Louis Charles Pineton de Chambrun, are so tangential that it was thought unnecessary to list them in an abbreviated bibliography. They are, however, clearly cited, and can be easily consulted.

INDEX